the 1950s

RECORDED VERSIONS GUITAR

ISBN 0-634-04066-9

HAL•LEONARD®
CORPORATION

7777 W. BLUEMOUND RD. P.O. BOX 13819 MILWAUKEE, WI 53213

Visit Hal Leonard Online at
www.halleonard.com

the 1950s

CONTENTS

All Shook Up

Words and Music by Otis Blackwell and Elvis Presley

Additional Lyrics

3.,4. When she touched my hand, oh what a chill I got.
Her lips were like a volcano and it's hot.
I'm proud to say that she's my buttercup.

Be-Bop-a-Lula

Words and Music by Tex Davis and Gene Vincent

* Played as even eighth notes.

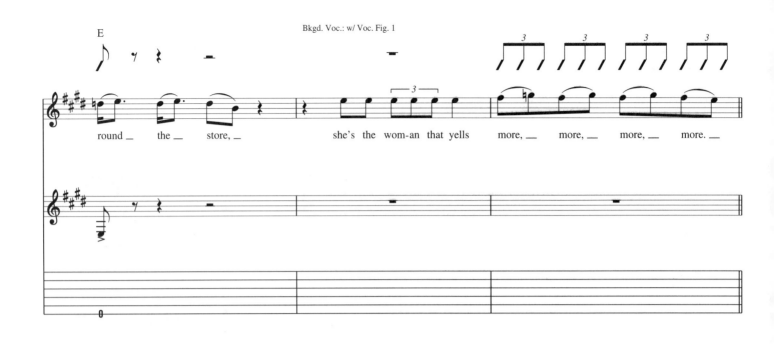

round __ the __ store, __ she's the wom-an that yells more, __ more, __ more, __ more. __

Chorus

Be - Bop - a - Lu - la, she's my __ ba - by. Be - Bop - a - Lu - la, I

w/ pick & fingers

don't __ mean __ may - be. Be - Bop - a - Lu - la, she - e - 's __ my ba - by

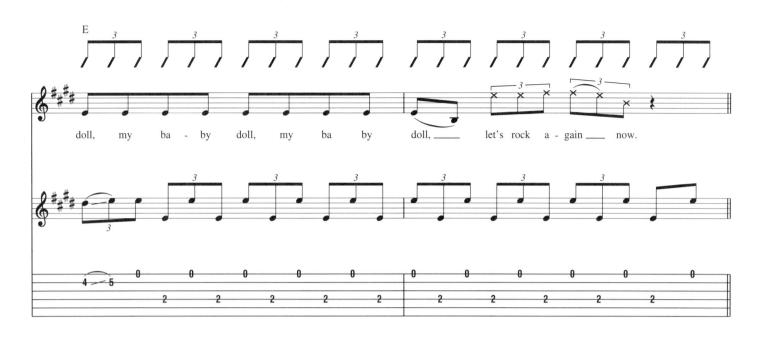

doll, my ba - by doll, my ba - by doll, ____ let's rock a - gain ____ now.

Guitar Solo

Gtr. 1: w/ Rhy. Fig. 1

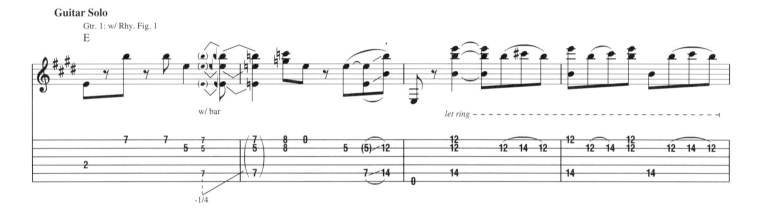

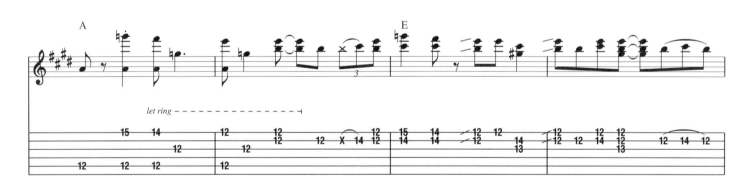

Well, ____ Be -

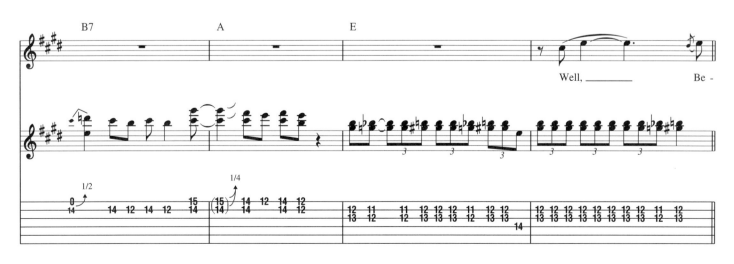

Bo Diddley

Words and Music by Ellas McDaniel

Bo Did-dle-y caught a bear-cat, _ to make his pret-ty ba-by a Sun-day hat. _

Guitar Solo

semi-mute

end muting

(A9) (G)

semi-mute

C Eb C

G

let chords ring

semi-mute

C

D(add4) C

G

Let chords ring

semi-mute

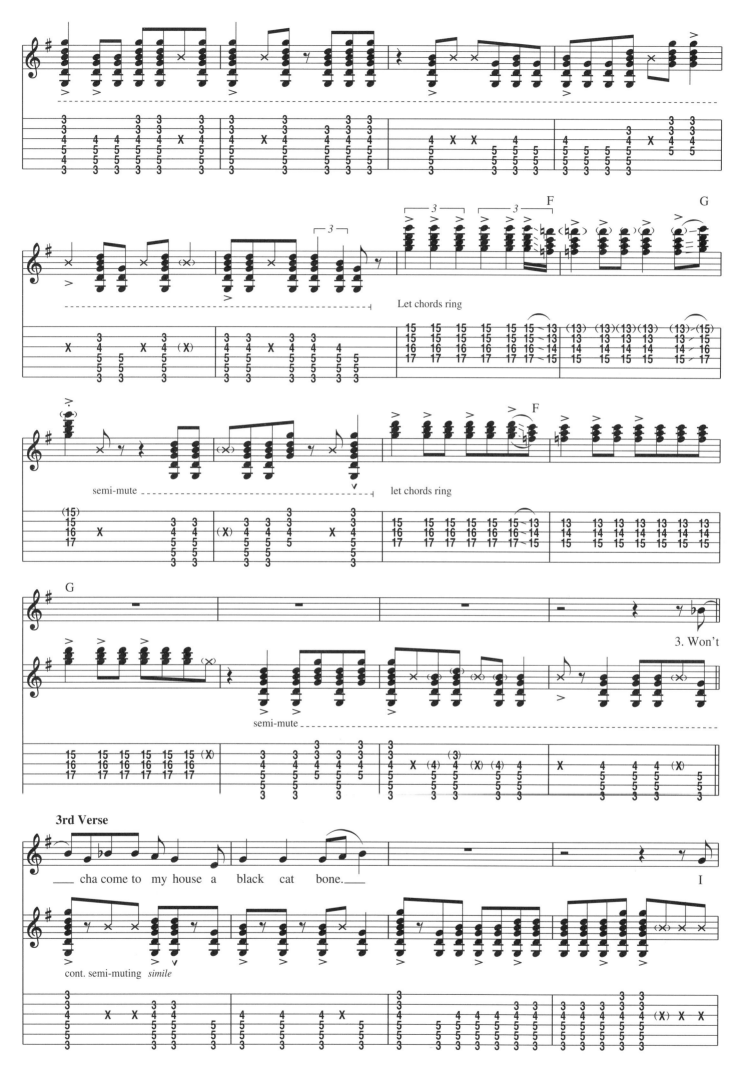

take my___ ba-by a - way from home.___

Cov-er that mo-jo an' where's he been? _____

up yo' house 'n' gone ___ a - gain. ___

Bo Did - dle-y, Bo Did-dle-y,

18

have   you heard?_____   My_

___ pur - ty ba - by that   she was mur-der - ed

Guitar Solo

(G#)   (G)

semi-muted _ _ _ _ _ _ _ _ _ _ _

(Gb)   (G)

semi-muted _ _ _ _ _ _ _ _ _ _   semi-muted _ _ _ _ _ _ _ _ _ _

Gsus4   G

_ _ _ _ _ _ _ _ _ _ _ _ _ _ _ _   semi-muted _ _ _ _ _ _ _ _ _ _ _ _ _

F#   G   E   F   G   *Fade Out*

Boppin' the Blues

Words and Music by Howard Griffin and Carl Perkins

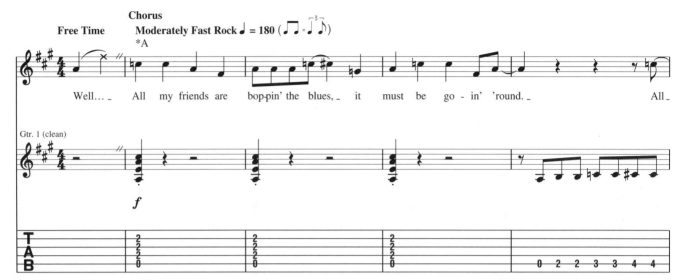

*Chord symbols reflect overall tonality.

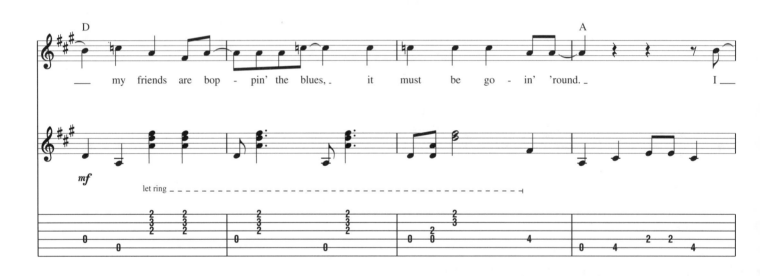

* Hold this note through 1st beat of repeat.

Coda 2

Outro

Gtr. 1: w/ Rhy. Fig. 1, simile

24

Cannonball

Words and Music by Duane Eddy and Lee Hazlewood

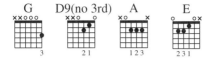

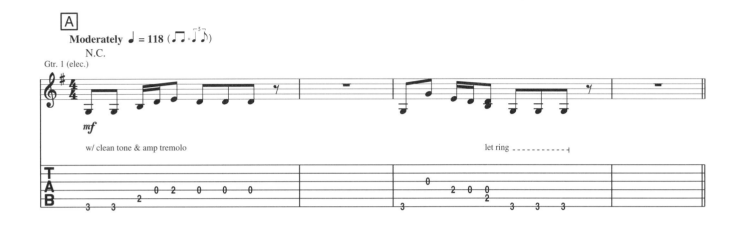

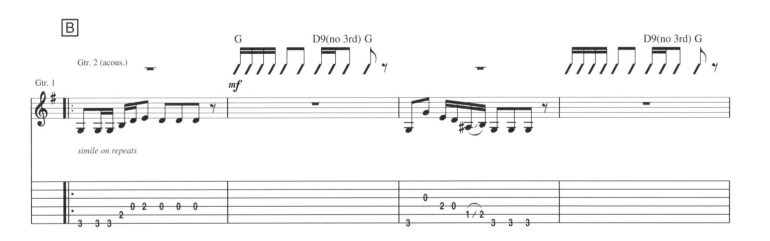

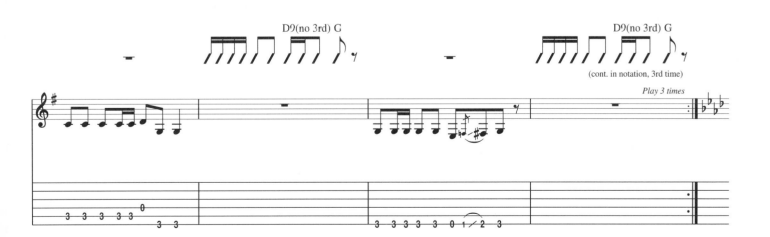

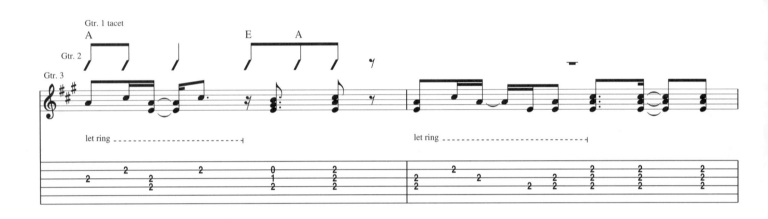

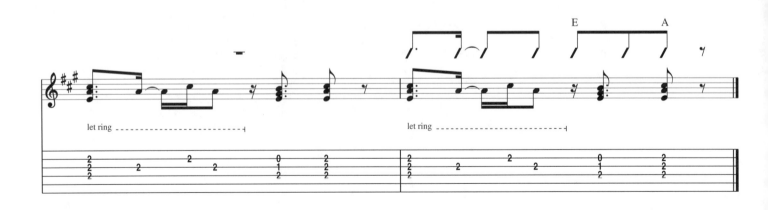

Donna

Words and Music by Ritchie Valens

Gtr. 2: w/ Rhy. Fig. 2 (3 times)

Since she left me, _____ I've nev - er _ been the same 'cause I love _____ my _ girl.

Don - na _____ where can you be, _____ where _ can _ you be?

Verse
Gtr. 1: w/ Rhy. Fig. 1 (3 times)
Gtr. 2: w/ Rhy. Fig. 2 (3 times)

2. Now _ that you're gone, _____ I'm left _____ all _____ a - lone.

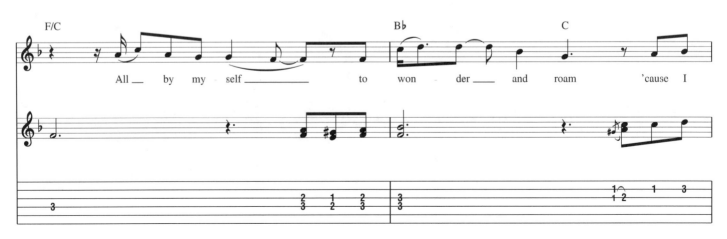

All _ by my self _____ to won der _ and roam 'cause I

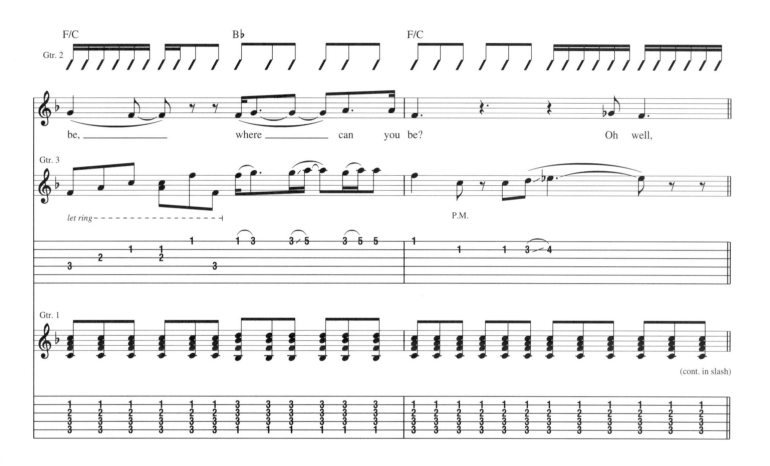

*Composite arrangement

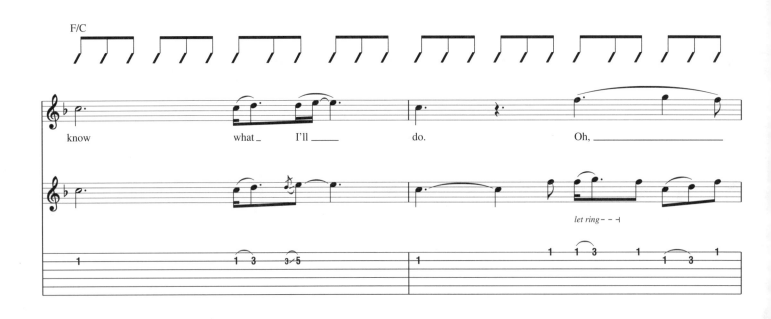

know   what_   I'll   do.   Oh, ___________

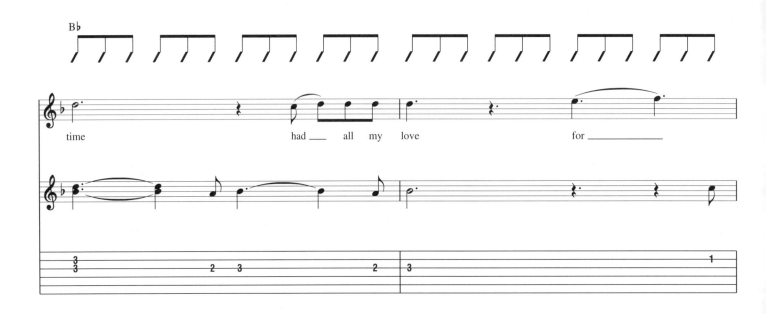

time   had_   all   my   love   for ______

you, _____________________   mm. ________

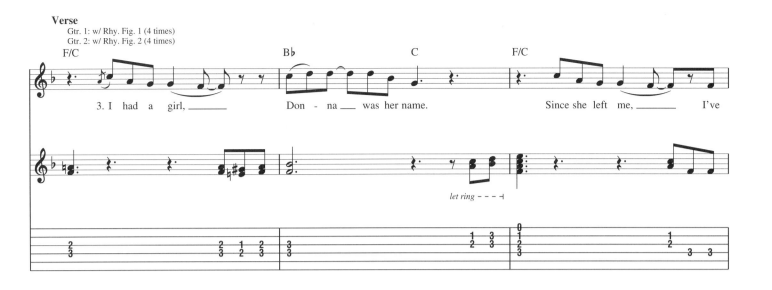

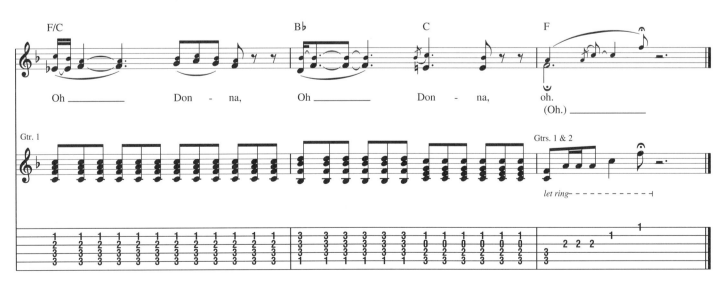

Foggy Mountain Breakdown

Words and Music by Earl Scruggs

*5th time

End Rhy. Fig. 1

35

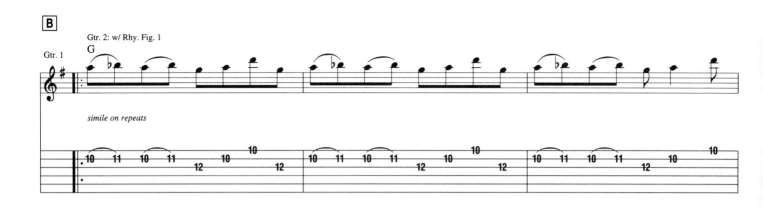

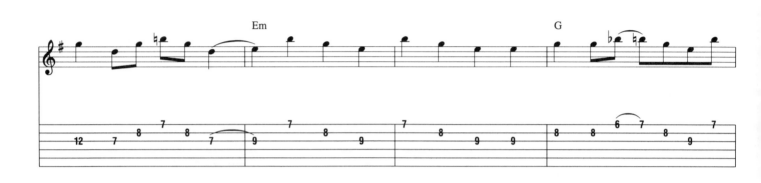

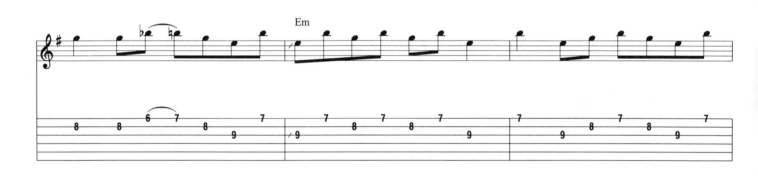

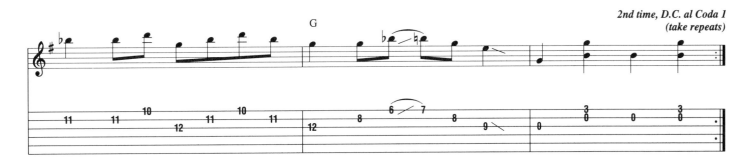

2nd time, D.C. al Coda 1
(take repeats)

Coda 1

D.C. al Coda 2
(no repeats)

Coda 2

Get Rhythm

Words and Music by John R. Cash

NOTE: Played with capo at 1st fret

E **Guitar Solo**

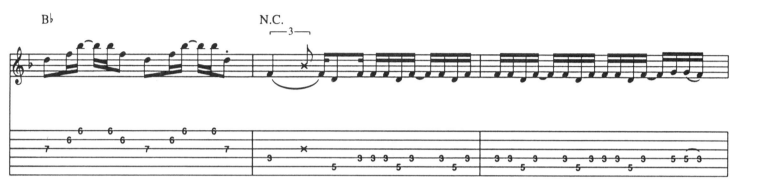

D.S. al Coda

Coda

Guitar Boogie Shuffle

By Arthur Smith

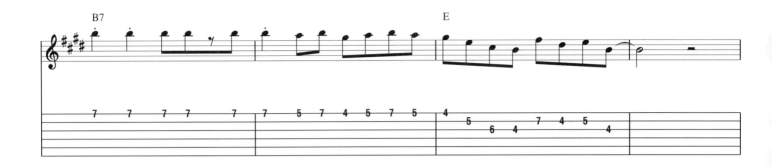

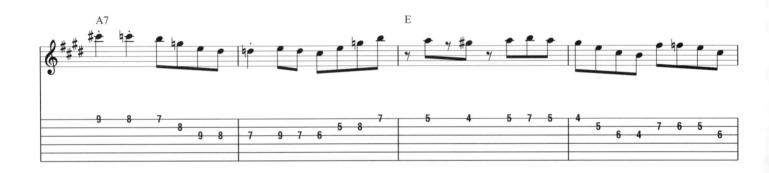

D.S. al Coda

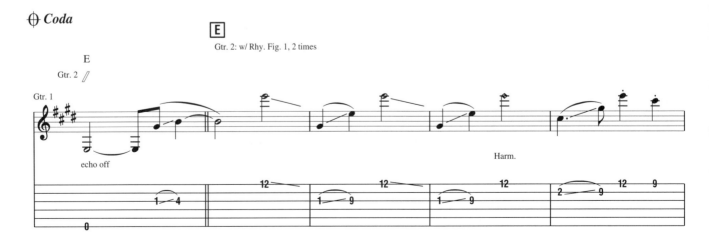

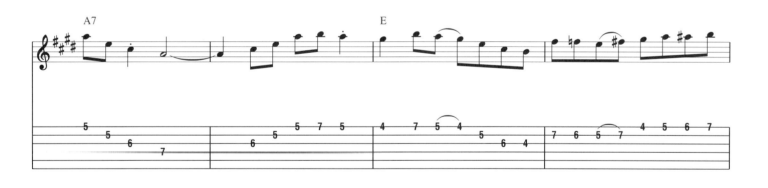

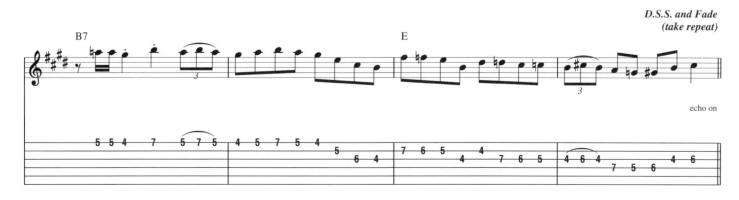

D.S.S. and Fade
(take repeat)

echo on

Heartbreak Hotel

Words and Music by Mae Boren Axton, Tommy Durden and Elvis Presley

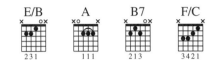

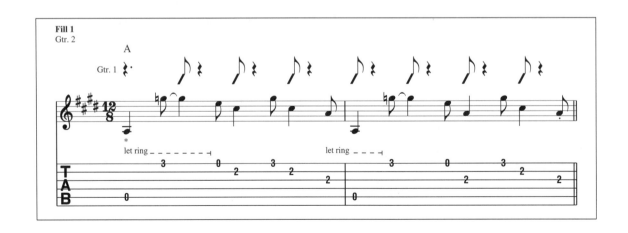

Gtrs. 1 & 2: w/ Fill 2, 2nd time

I'll be so lone - ly ____ I could die.
well, they're so lone - ly ____ they could die.

2. Al -
3. Now, the

Verse

E/B

Rhy. Fig. 1 / End Rhy. Fig. 1

bell - hop's tears keep flow - ing, the desk clerk's _ dressed in black. They've
though it's al - ways crowd - ed, you still can find ____ some room for

Rhy. Fig. 1A / End Rhy. Fig. 1A

To Coda

A

been so long ____ on Lone - ly Street they'll nev - er, nev - er look back. And they're so,
brok - en - heart - ed lov - ers to cry there in the gloom. We'll be so,

Gtr. 2: w/ Fill 3, 2nd time

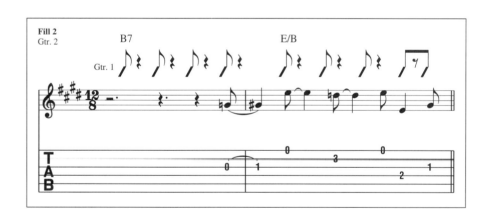

Fill 2
Gtr. 2

B7   E/B

Gtr. 1

Fill 3
Gtr. 2

8va

and they're so lone-ly, ba-by, well, they're so lone-ly,

well, they're so lone-ly ___ they could die. 4. Well, ___ now

Verse

Gtrs. 1 & 2: w/ Rhy. Figs. 1 & 1A

if you're ___ ba-by leaves ___ you and you've got a tale ___ to tell, well, just

take a walk ___ down Lone-ly Street to Heart-break Ho-tel ___ where you will be,

Hound Dog

Words and Music by Jerry Leiber and Mike Stoller

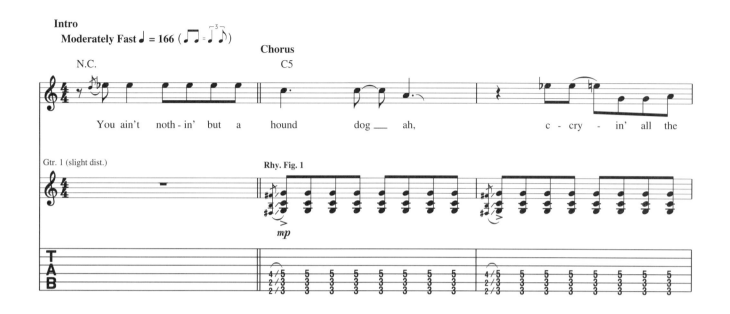

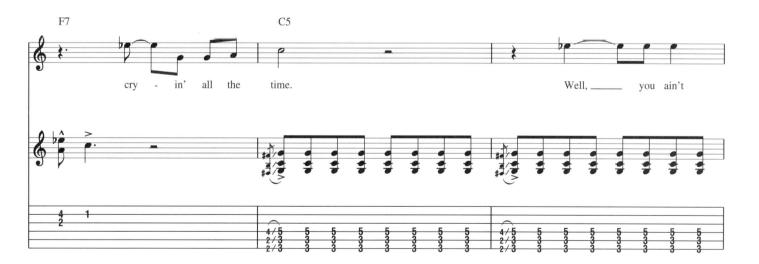

Verse

Gtr. 1: w/ Rhy. Fig. 1, simile

Chorus

Gtr. 1: w/ Rhy. Fig. 1, 1st 11 meas., simile

Guitar Solo

* Chord symbols reflect implied tonality.

D.S. al Coda 1

2. Well, they said you was high

53

I'm Lookin' for Someone to Love

Words and Music by Buddy Holly and Norman Petty

I'm Movin' On

Words and Music by Hank Snow

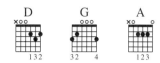

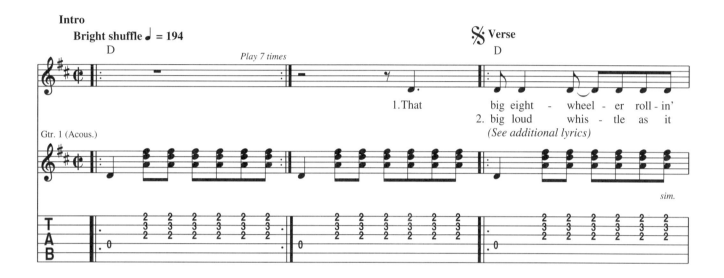

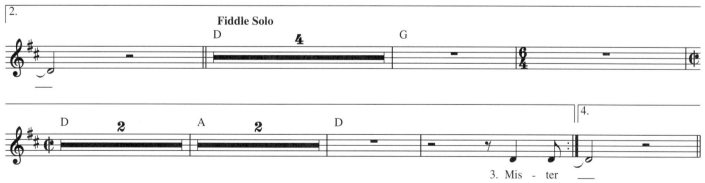

Guitar Solo

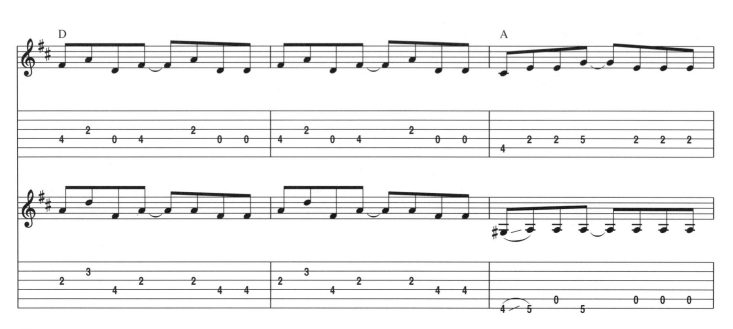

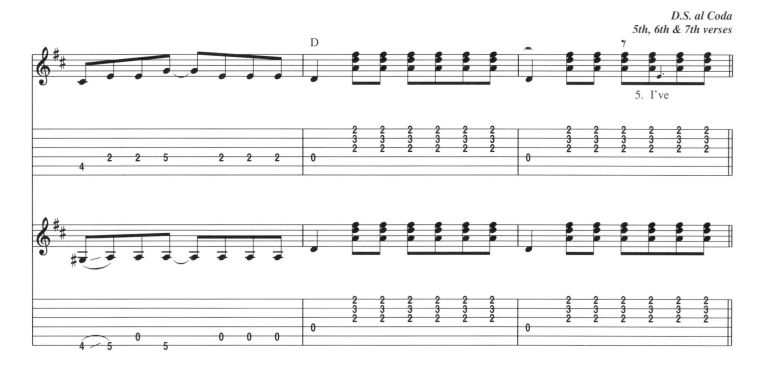

Coda

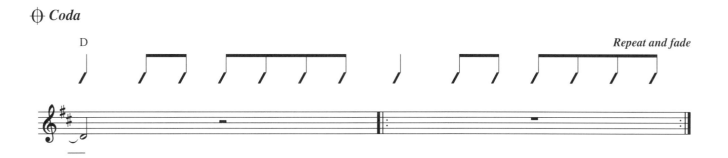

Additional Lyrics

3. Mister fireman, won't you listen to me,
   'cause I got a pretty mama in Tennessee.
   Keep movin' on, keep rollin' on.
   So shovel the coal, let this rattler roll and keep movin' me on.

4. Mister engineer, take that throttle in hand,
   this rattler's the fastest in the southern land.
   Keep movin' me on, keep rollin' on.
   You're gonna ease my mind, put me there on time and keep rollin' on. *(Guitar solo)*

5. I've told you, baby, from time to time,
   but you just wouldn't listen or pay me no mind,
   Now I'm movin' on, I'm rollin' on.
   You've broken your vow and it's all over now, so I'm movin' on.

6. You switched your engine, now I ain't got time
   for a triflin' woman on my main line,
   'cause I'm movin' on. You've done your daddy wrong.
   I've warned you twice, now you can saddle the price, 'cause I'm movin' on.

7. But someday, baby, when you've had your play,
   you're gonna want your daddy, but your daddy will say:
   "Keep movin' on. You stayed away too long.
   I'm through with you, too bad you're blue, keep movin' on."

I'm Your Hoochie Coochie Man

Written by Willie Dixon

Lonesome Town

Words and Music by Baker Knight

Tune down 1/2 step:
(low to high) Eb–Ab–Db–Gb–Bb–Eb

Intro

Slowly ♩ = 77

*Chord symbols reflect basic harmony.

% Verse

1. There's a place where lov-ers go ___ to
2. You can buy a dream or two
3. In the town of bro-ken dreams, ___

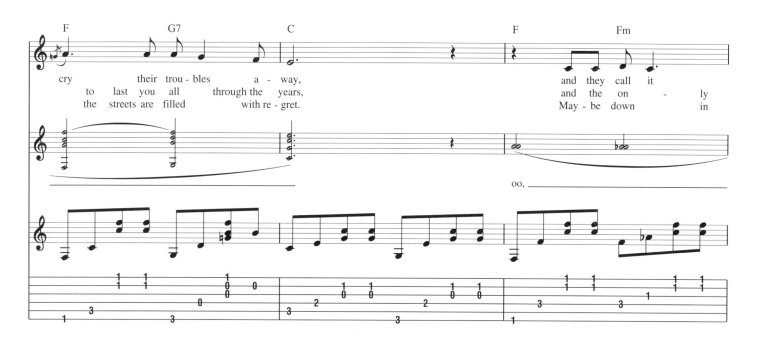

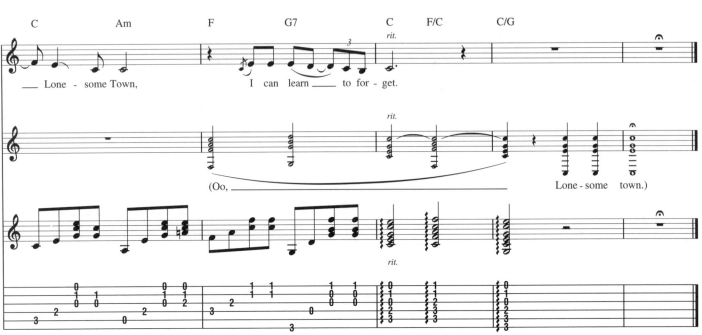

Matchbox

Words and Music by Carl Lee Perkins

Guitar Solo

Verse

Moonlight in Vermont

Words and Music by John Blackburn and Karl Suessdorf

* Chord symbols reflect implied tonality.

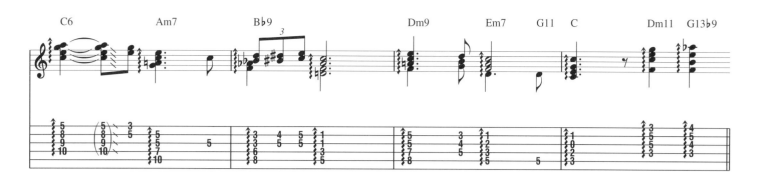

B Alto Sax Solo

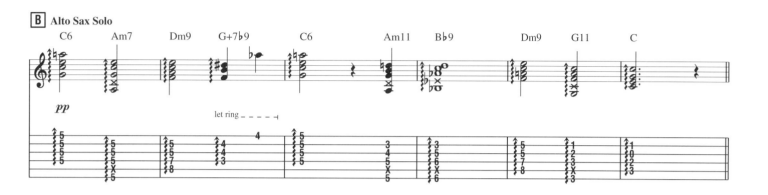

C Guitar Solo
Rubato

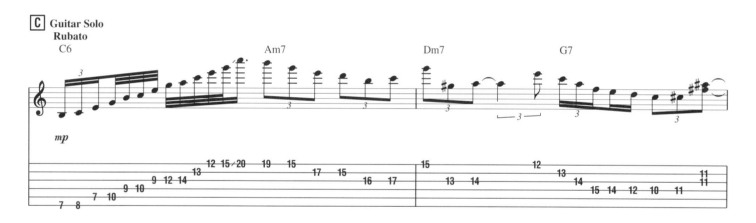

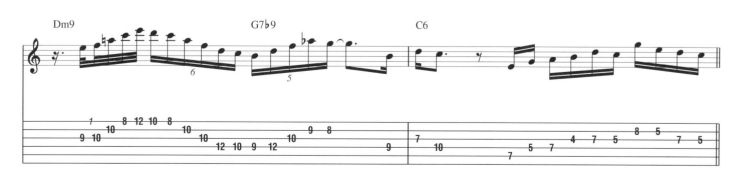

My Babe

Written by Willie Dixon

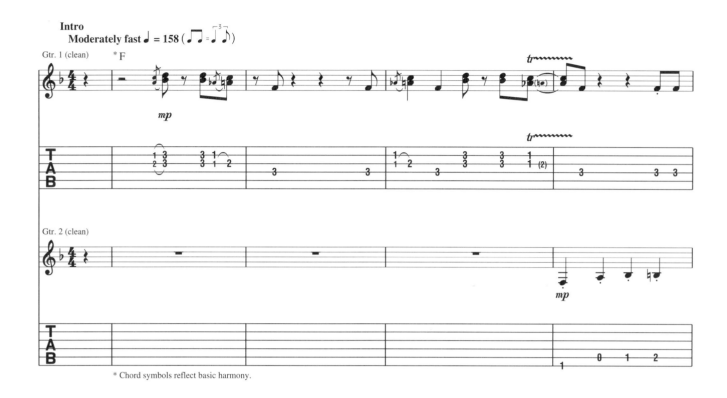

* Chord symbols reflect basic harmony.

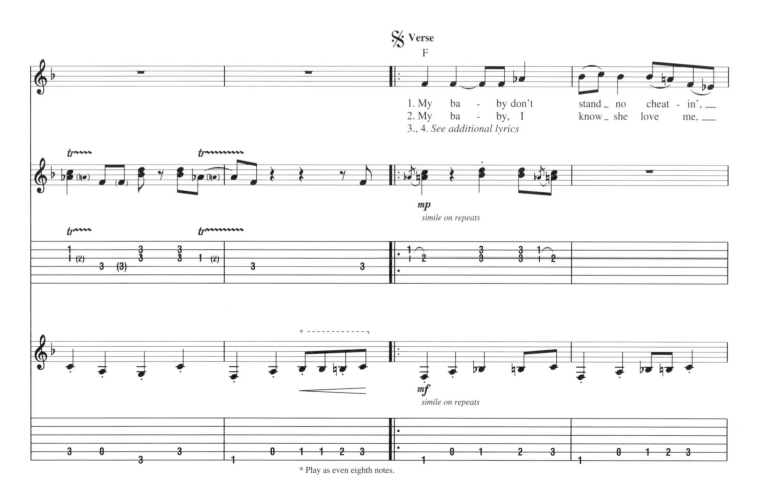

* Play as even eighth notes.

don't __ stand __ none o' that mid - night creep - in'. _____ My babe, true __
don't __ do ____ nut - tin' but kiss an' hug __ me. My babe, true __

4th time, to Coda

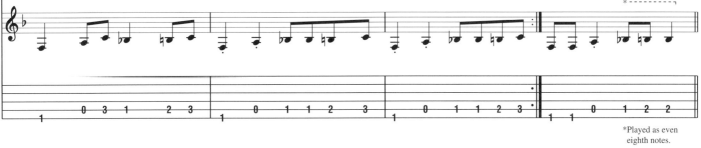

1.
3rd time, Gtr. 1: w/ Fill 1

2.

__ lit - tle ba - by, __ mm, my babe.
__ lit - tle ba - by, __ mm, my babe.

*Played as even eighth notes.

Fill 1
Gtr. 1

Harmonica Solo

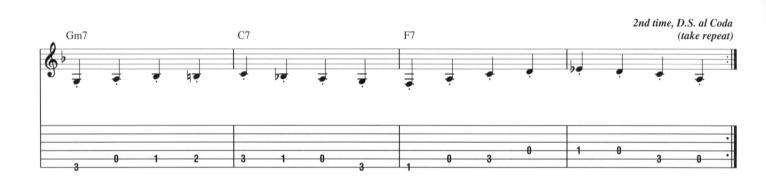

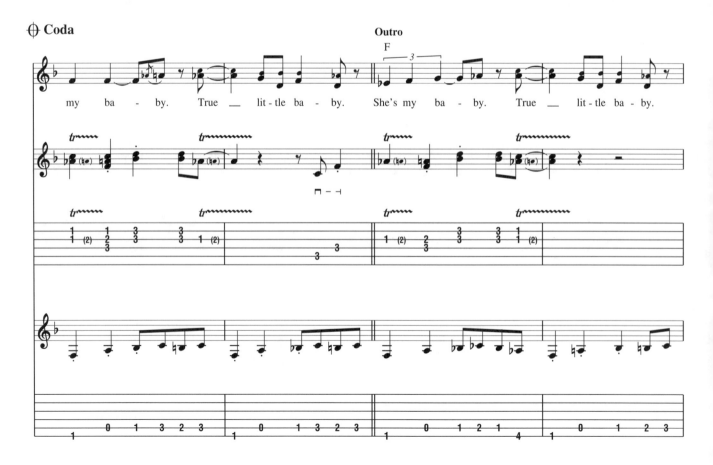

Additional Lyrics

3. My baby don't stand no cheatin', my babe.
   Oh no, she don't stand no cheatin', my baby.
   Oh no, she don't stand no cheatin',
   Ev'rything she do, she do so pleasin'.
   My babe, true little baby, my babe.

4. My baby don't stand no foolin', my babe.
   Oh yeah, she don't stand no foolin', my baby.
   Oh yeah, she don't stand no foolin',
   When she's hot, there ain't no coolin'.
   My babe, true little baby, she's my baby.
   True little baby.

Poor Little Fool

Words and Music by Sharon Sheeley

Chorus
Bkgd. Voc.: w/ Voc. Fig. 1
Gtrs. 1 & 2: w/ Rhy. Figs. 1 & 1A

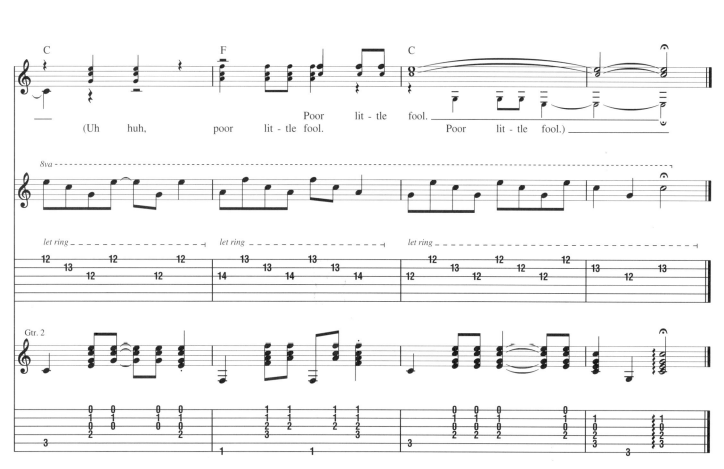

Additional Lyrics

4. The next day she was gone and I knew she lied to me.
   She left me with a broken heart and won her victory.

5. Well, I've played this game with other hearts, but I never thought I'd see
   The day when someone else would play love's foolish game with me.

Put Your Cat Clothes On

By Carl Perkins

cat clothes on __ 'cause to-night we're gon-na, gon-na __ bop it right. __   Scat, cat!

E Guitar Solo

* w/echo

* Tape echo device set for "slapback" delay.

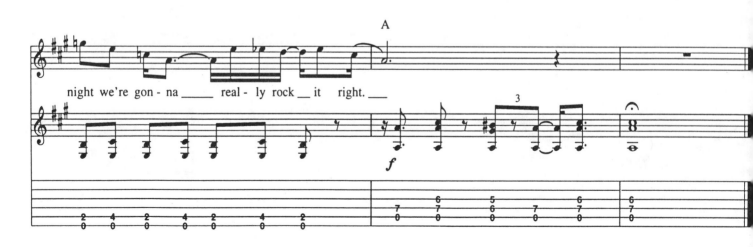

Race With the Devil

By Gene Vincent

E Guitar Solo

gain!

N.C. (B♭)

N.C. (F)   N.C. (C)   N.C. (B♭)

N.C. (F)   F Verse

F5   F⁶₉

5. I was   do-in' pret-ty fine,   I
     I've led an e-vil life,

(1st time only)

F5   E♭5   D5   C5

looked up be-hind, __   uh,   here come   the Dev-il   do-in'   nine-ty nine. __   Sing-in'
so they say,   but I'll   hide from   the Dev-il   on   Judge-ment day.

Rebel 'Rouser

By Duane Eddy and Lee Hazlewood

Reconsider Baby

Words and Music by Lowell Fulson

2.,3. *(See Additional Verses)*

oh, how I hate __ to see you go.__ And the way__

__ that I will miss you, __ I guess you will nev - er know. __ 2. We've been to-geth -

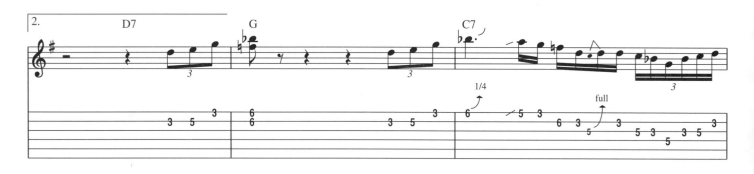

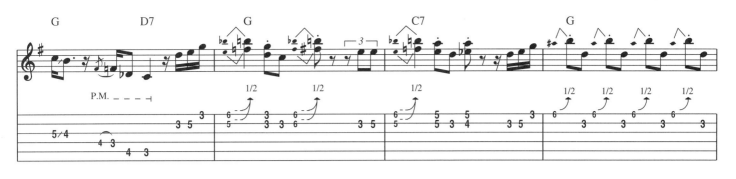

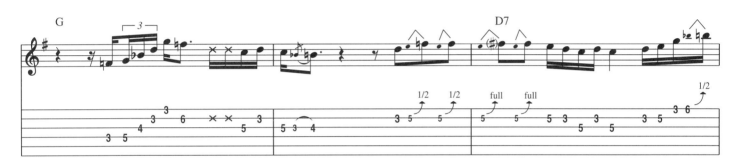

D.S. (3rd verse) al Coda

3. You said you once

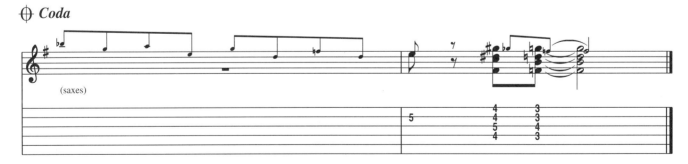

Additional Verses:

2. We've been together so long to have to separate this way.
   We've been together so long to have to separate this way.
   I'm gonna let you go ahead on, baby, pray that you'll come back home some day.

3. You said you once had loved me, but now I guess you have changed your mind.
   You said you once had loved me, but now I guess you have changed your mind.
   Why don't you reconsider, baby, give yourself just a little more time.

Rock Around the Clock

Words and Music by Max C. Freedman and Jimmy DeKnight

3. When the

Coda

Interlude

* Raise vol. as before.

D9

A

E9

Verse

A

5. When the clock strikes twelve, we'll cool off then, _ start a-

Additional Lyrics

3. When the chimes ring five, six and seven,
   We'll be right in seventh heaven.
   We're gonna around the clock tonight.
   We're gonna rock, rock, rock till broad daylight.
   We're gonna rock, gonna rock around the clock tonight.

4. When it's eight, nine, ten, eleven too,
   I'll be goin' strong and so will you.
   We're gonna around the clock tonight.
   We're gonna rock, rock, rock till broad daylight.
   We're gonna rock, gonna rock around the clock tonight.

Rocket '88

Words and Music by Jackie Brenston

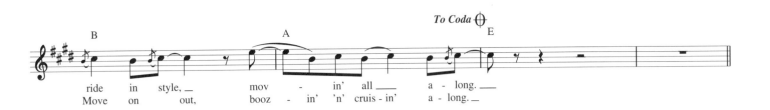

ride in style, ___ mov - in' all ___ a - long. ___
Move on out, booz - in' 'n' cruis - in' a - long. ___

Interlude

Gtr. 1: w/ Riff A

* Gtr. 2

* Tenor saxophones arr. for gtr.

Verse

Gtr. 1: w/ Riff A (1st 8 meas.)
Gtr. 2 tacet

2. V - eight mo - tor 'n' this smart ___ 'n' de - sign, black con - vert - a - ble top ___ an' the gals ___

___ don't ___ mind. ___ Sport - in' with me, rid - in' all ____ 'round __ town __ for joy. ___

Sax Solo

Gtr. 1: w/ Rhy. Fig. 1 (3 times), simile

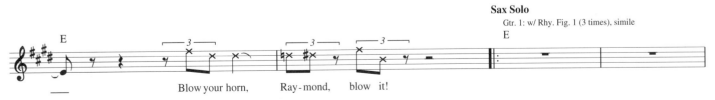

___ Blow your horn, Ray - mond, blow it!

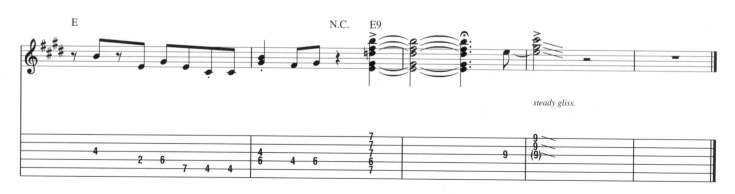

Rockin' Robin

Words and Music by J. Thomas

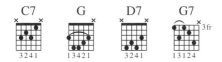

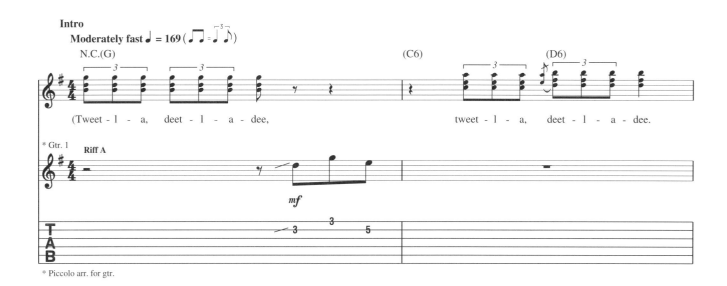

* Piccolo arr. for gtr.

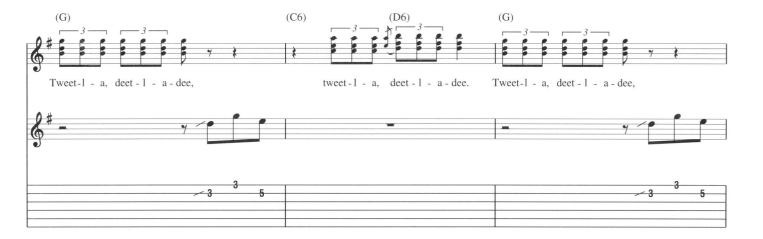

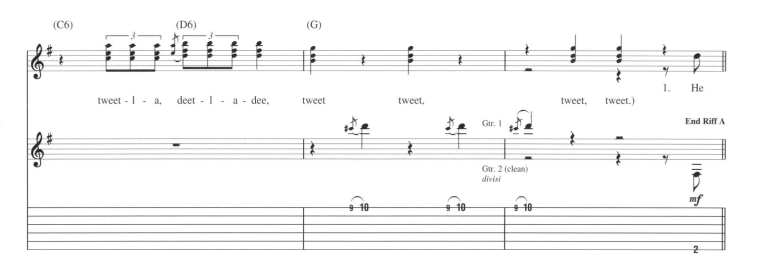

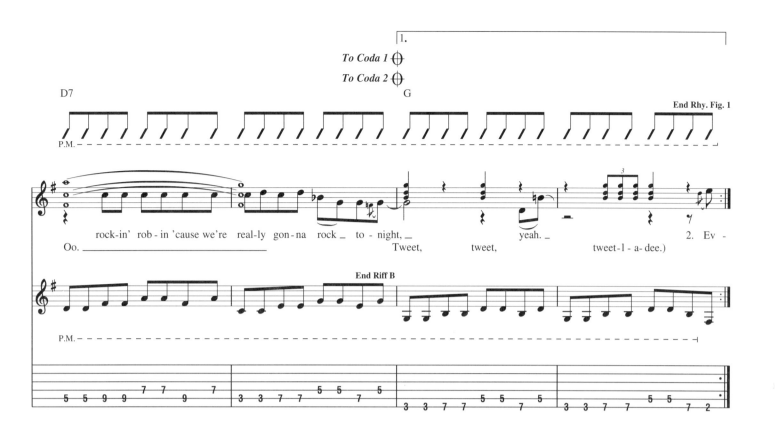

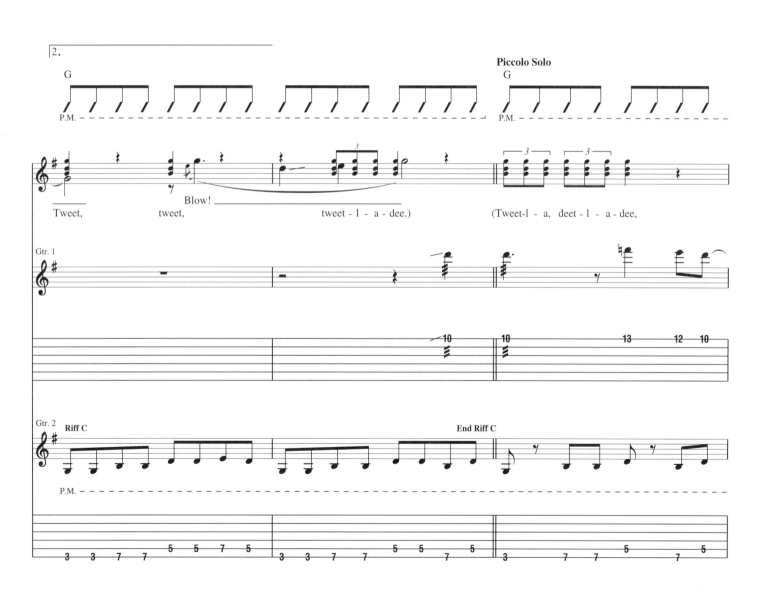

Coda 1

Gtr. 2: w/ Riff C
Gtr. 3: w/ Rhy. Fig. 1 (last 2 meas.)

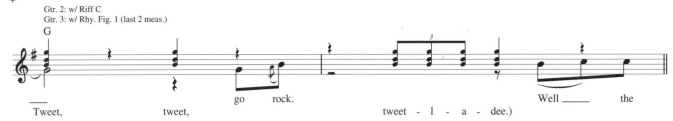

Tweet,   tweet,   go rock.   tweet - l - a - dee.)   Well ___ the

Bridge

Gtr. 2: w/ Riff D
Gtr. 3: w/ Rhy. Fig. 2

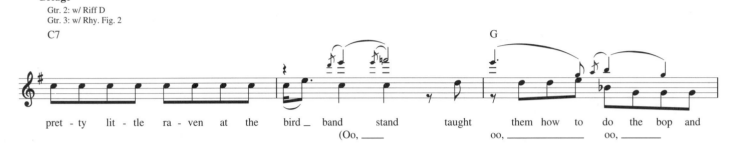

pret - ty lit - tle ra - ven at the bird ___ band stand taught them how to do the bop and
(Oo, ___   oo, ___   oo, ___

it ___ was grand. They start - ed go - ing stead - y and bless ___ my soul, he
oo, ___   oo, ___   oo.) ___

D.S. al Coda 2
(take 1st lyrics)

out bopped the buz - zard and the or - i - ole. ___ He

Coda 2

Gtr. 2: w/ Riff C
Gtr. 3: w/ Rhy. Fig. 1 (last 2 meas.)

Outro

Gtr. 1: w/ Riff A

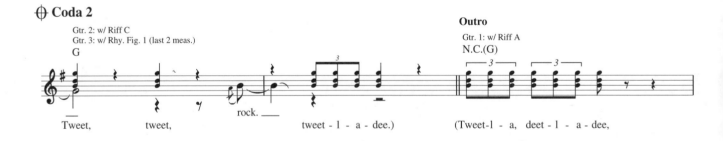

Tweet,   tweet,   rock. ___   tweet - l - a - dee.)   (Tweet-l - a, deet - l - a - dee,

tweet - l - a, deet - l - a - dee.   Tweet l - a, deet - l - a - dee,   tweet - l - a, deet - l - a - dee.

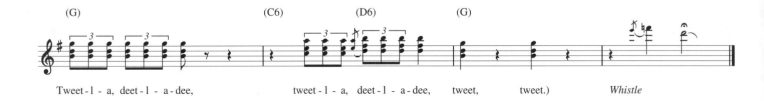

Tweet - l - a, deet - l - a - dee,   tweet - l - a, deet - l - a - dee,   tweet,   tweet.)   *Whistle*

Sleepwalk

By Santo Farina, John Farina and Ann Farina

Slippin' and Slidin'

Words and Music by Richard Penniman, Edwin Bocage, Albert Collins and James Smith

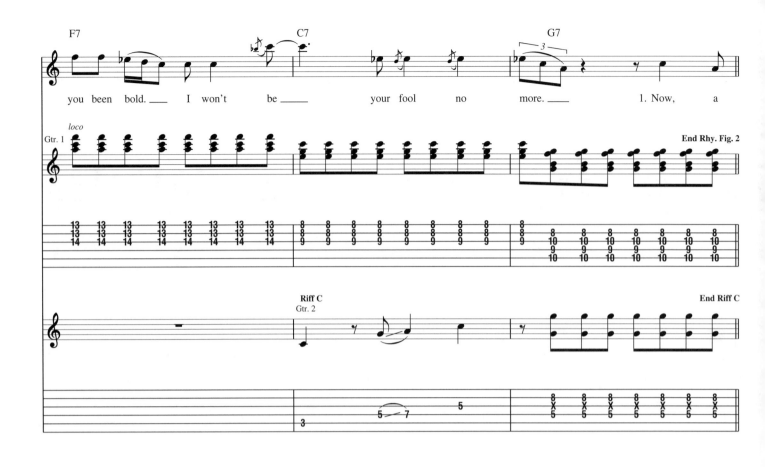

you been bold. ___ I won't be _____ your fool no more. ___ 1. Now, a

Gtr. 1 *loco*

End Rhy. Fig. 2

Riff C
Gtr. 2

End Riff C

Verse
Gtr. 1: w/ Rhy. Fig. 1
Gtr. 2: w/ Riff B

ho, big con-niv-er, he's noth-in' but a jiv-er. I done got hip to your jive. _____ Now, a

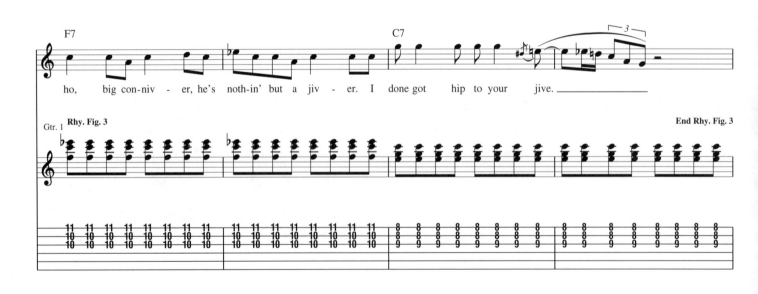

ho, big con-niv-er, he's noth-in' but a jiv-er. I done got hip to your jive. _____

Gtr. 1 **Rhy. Fig. 3**

End Rhy. Fig. 3

Gtr. 1: w/ Rhy. Fig. 2

Gtr. 2: w/ Riff C

D.S. al Coda 1

Slip-pin' and a slid-in', peep-in' and a hid-in'. Won't be your fool __ no more. __ Now I'm

old Ma - lin - da, she's a sol - id sin - ner. You know you bet - ter sur - ren - der. _____

Slip-pin' and a slid - in', peep-in' and hid - in'. Won't be ___ your fool no ___ more. ___ Now, I'm

⊕ Coda 2

Gtr. 1: w/ Rhy. Fig. 2

Gtr. 2: w/ Riff C

I been told, ___ ba - by you been bold. ___ I won't be ___ your fool no ___ more. Ow, _____ woo!

Saxophone Solo

Gtr. 1: w/ Riff A

Gtr. 2

* Played behind the beat.

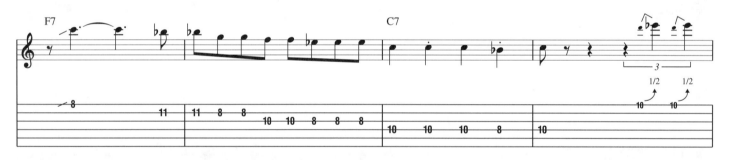

Outro   *Begin fade*   *Fade out*

Gtr. 1: w/ Rhy. Fig. 1

Gtr. 1: w/ Rhy. Fig. 2 (1st meas.)

Susie-Q

Words and Music by Dale Hawkins, Stan Lewis and Eleanor Broadwater

Verse

C7　　　B7　　　E7　　　　　　　　　　　　　　　　E7

__ my Su - zie Q. __　　　　　　　　　2. I like the way　　you walk. __
__ my Su - zie Q. __　　　　　　　　　4. Well, say that you'll　be true. __

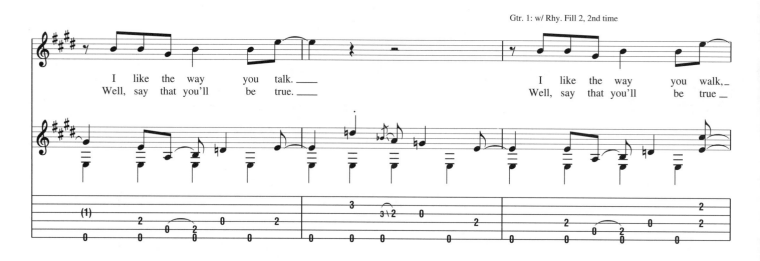

Gtr. 1: w/ Rhy. Fill 2, 2nd time

I like the way　　you talk. __　　　　　　I like the way　　　you walk,_
Well, say that you'll　be true. __　　　　Well, say that you'll　　be true _

A7　　　　　　　　C7　　　B7　　　E7　　　　　To Coda ⊕

__ I like the way you　talk, __ my Su - zie　Q. __
__ and nev - er leave me　blue, __ my Su - zie　Q. __

w/ pick

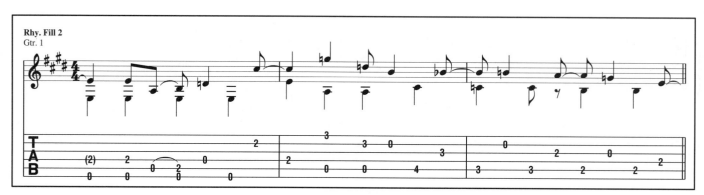

Rhy. Fill 2
Gtr. 1

120

* 1st string sounded by pull-off.

Sweet Little Angel

Words and Music by B.B. King and Jules Bihari

* Chord symbols reflect overall tonality.

Tequila

By Chuck Rio

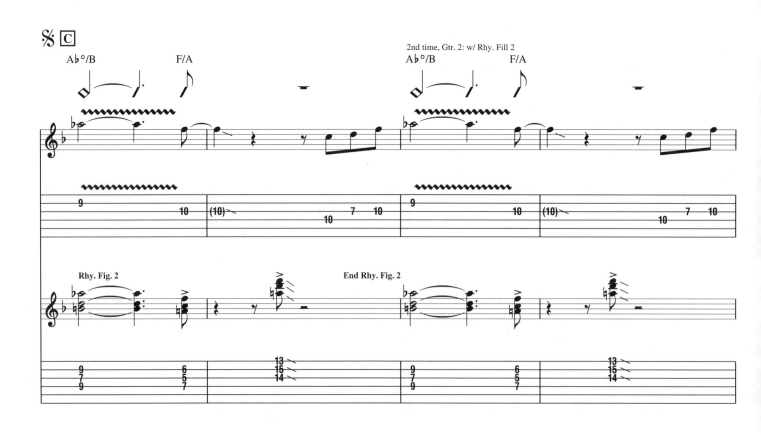

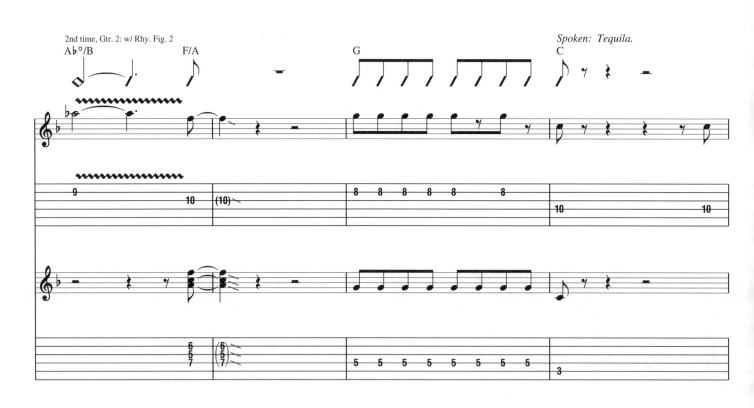

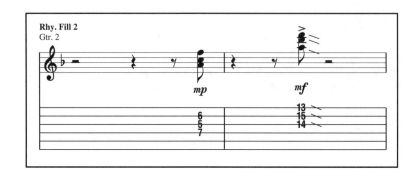

(They Call It) Stormy Monday

(Stormy Monday Blues)

Words and Music by Aaron "T-Bone" Walker

* Chord symbols reflect overall tonality.

*** Played as even eighth notes.

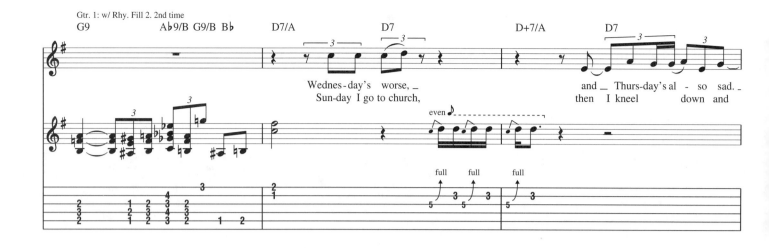

Gtr. 1: w/ Rhy. Fill 2. 2nd time

Wednes-day's worse, ___
Sun-day I go to church,

and ___ Thurs-day's al - so sad.
then I kneel down and

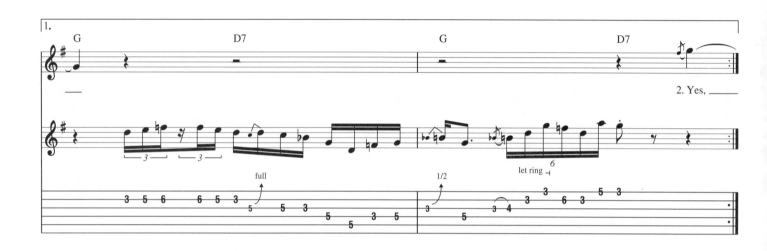

1.

2. Yes, ___

pray.

2.

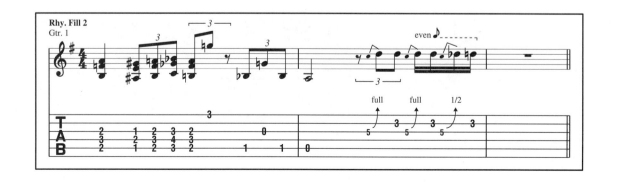

Rhy. Fill 2
Gtr. 1

Lord have mer-cy,

my heart's in mis-er-y.

Cra-zy 'bout my ba-by,

yeah, _____ send her back to me. ___

* Played behind the beat.

Wake Up Little Susie

Words and Music by Boudleaux Bryant and Felice Bryant

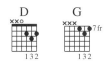

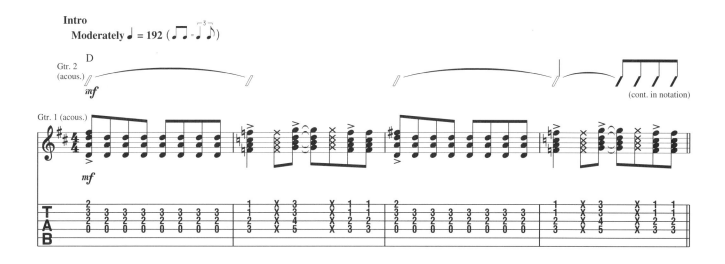

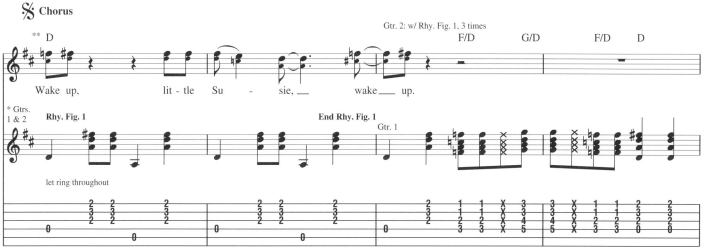

* composite arrangement

** Chord symbols reflect overall tonality.

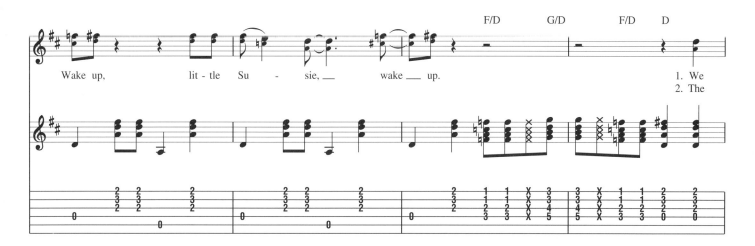

Verse

what-'re we gon-na tell your ma - ma? What-'re we gon-na tell your pa? ___

Gtr. 3 tacet

What-'re we gon-na tell our friends ___ when they say, "Ooh, la,

Gtrs. 1 & 2

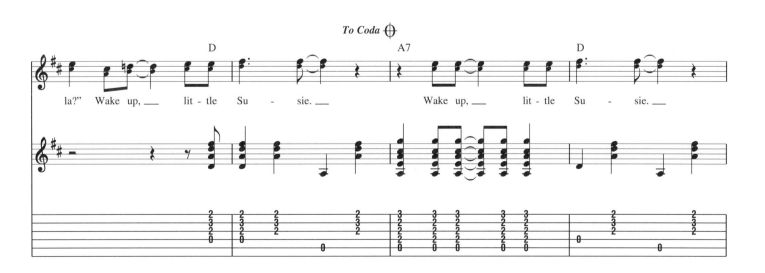

To Coda ⊕

la?" Wake up, ___ lit - tle Su - sie. ___ Wake up, ___ lit - tle Su - sie. ___

The World Is Waiting for the Sunrise

Words by Eugene Lockhart
Music by Ernest Seitz

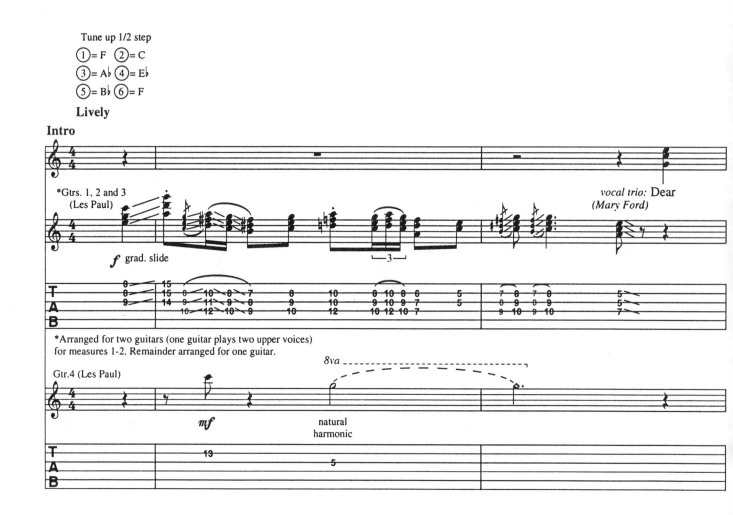

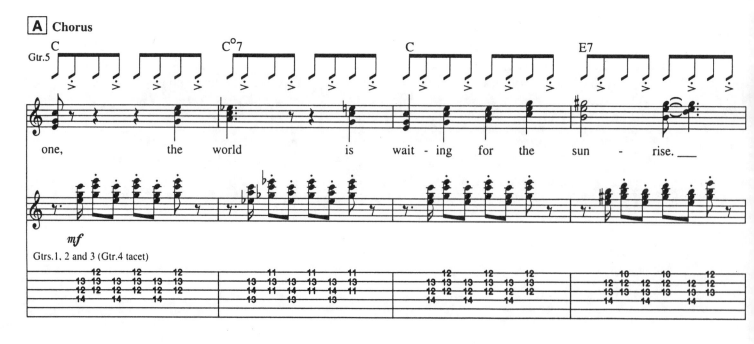

B Guitar Solo

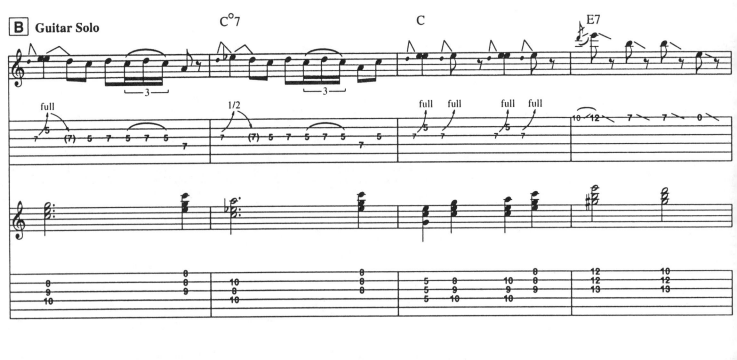

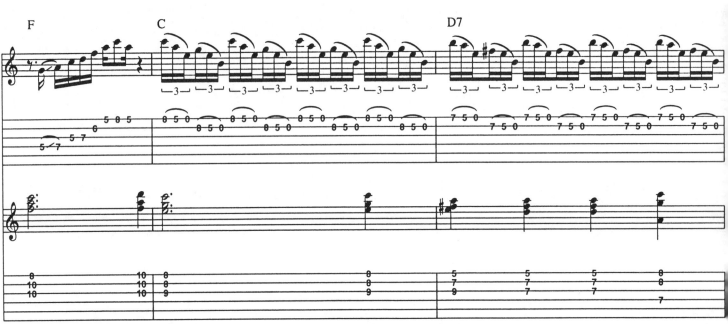

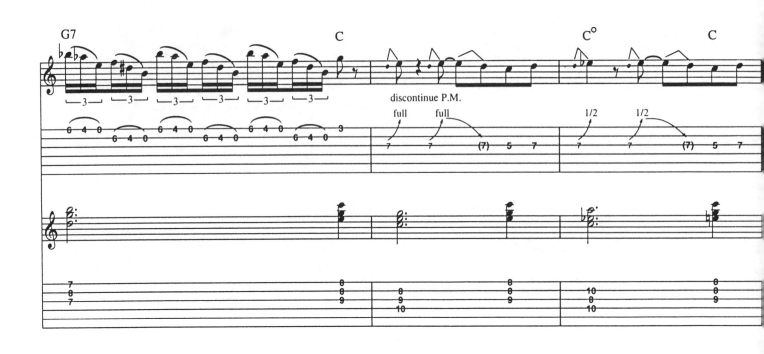

148

Yankee Doodle Dixie

By Chet Atkins

* Chord symbols reflect basic harmony.

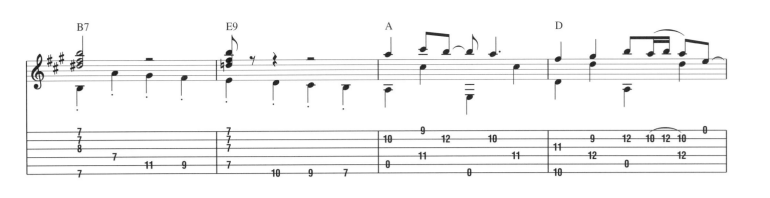

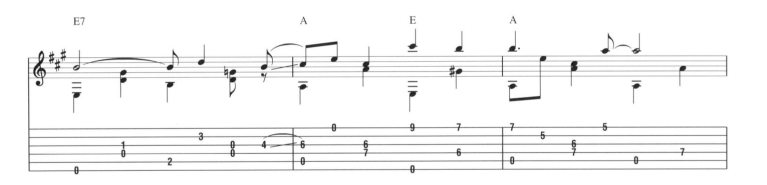

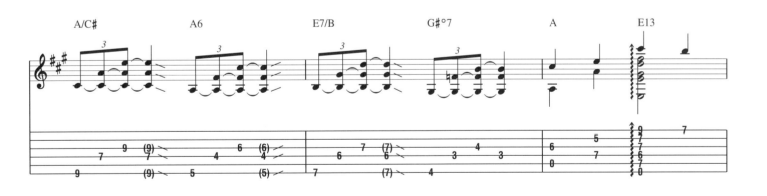

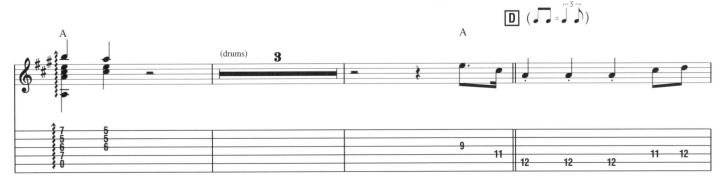

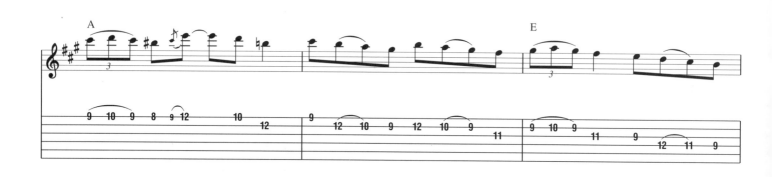

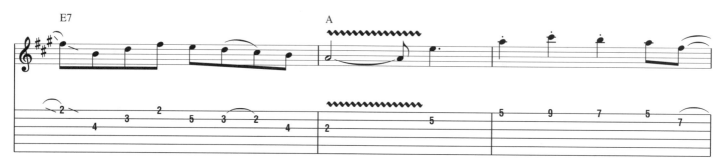

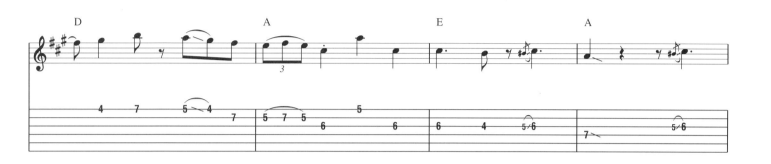

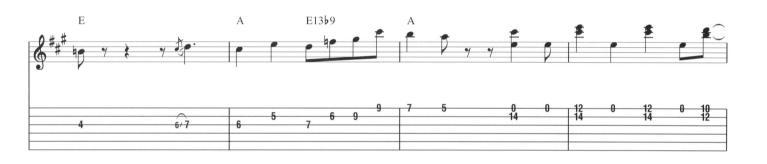

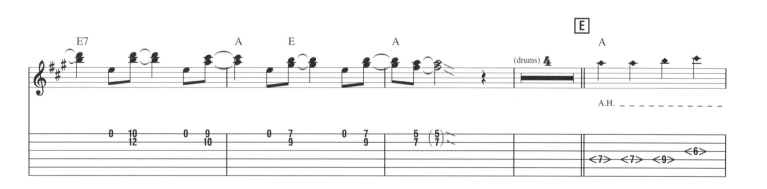

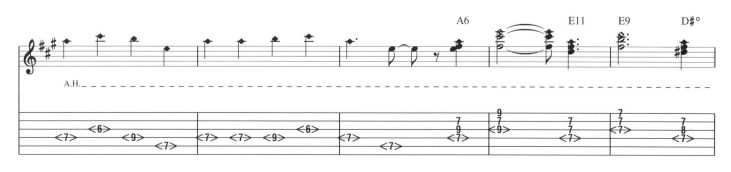

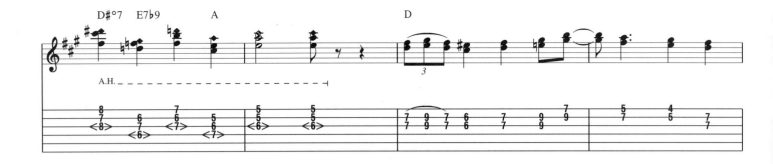

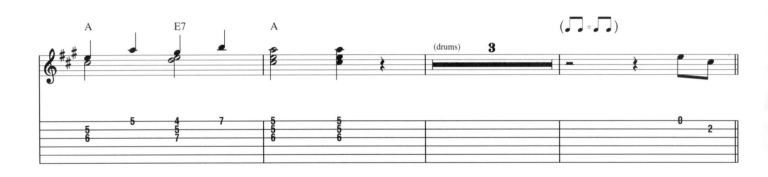

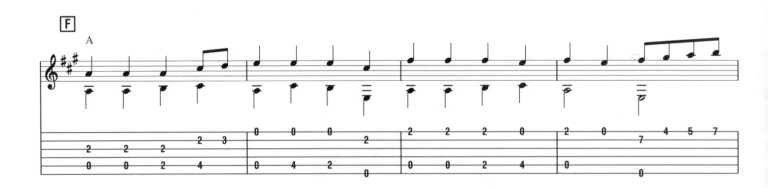

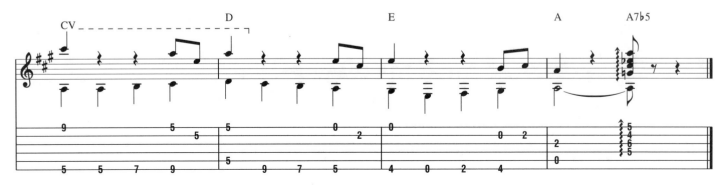

Guitar Notation Legend

Guitar Music can be notated three different ways: on a *musical staff*, in *tablature*, and in *rhythm slashes*.

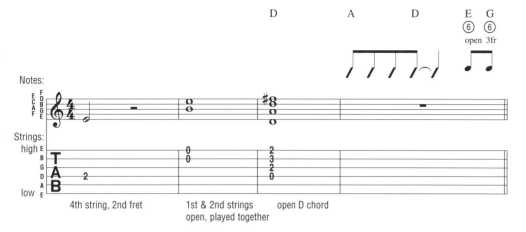

RHYTHM SLASHES are written above the staff. Strum chords in the rhythm indicated. Use the chord diagrams found at the top of the first page of the transcription for the appropriate chord voicings. Round noteheads indicate single notes.

THE MUSICAL STAFF shows pitches and rhythms and is divided by bar lines into measures. Pitches are named after the first seven letters of the alphabet.

TABLATURE graphically represents the guitar fingerboard. Each horizontal line represents a a string, and each number represents a fret.

4th string, 2nd fret   1st & 2nd strings open, played together   open D chord

Definitions for Special Guitar Notation

HALF-STEP BEND: Strike the note and bend up 1/2 step.

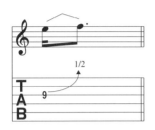

WHOLE-STEP BEND: Strike the note and bend up one step.

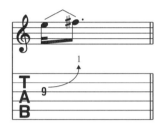

GRACE NOTE BEND: Strike the note and immediately bend up as indicated.

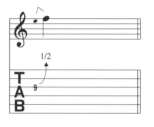

SLIGHT (MICROTONE) BEND: Strike the note and bend up 1/4 step.

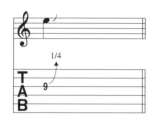

BEND AND RELEASE: Strike the note and bend up as indicated, then release back to the original note. Only the first note is struck.

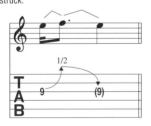

PRE-BEND: Bend the note as indicated, then strike it.

PRE-BEND AND RELEASE: Bend the note as indicated. Strike it and release the bend back to the original note.

UNISON BEND: Strike the two notes simultaneously and bend the lower note up to the pitch of the higher.

VIBRATO: The string is vibrated by rapidly bending and releasing the note with the fretting hand.

WIDE VIBRATO: The pitch is varied to a greater degree by vibrating with the fretting hand.

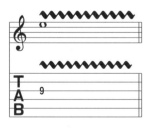

HAMMER-ON: Strike the first (lower) note with one finger, then sound the higher note (on the same string) with another finger by fretting it without picking.

PULL-OFF: Place both fingers on the notes to be sounded. Strike the first note and without picking, pull the finger off to sound the second (lower) note.

LEGATO SLIDE: Strike the first note and then slide the same fret-hand finger up or down to the second note. The second note is not struck.

SHIFT SLIDE: Same as legato slide, except the second note is struck.

TRILL: Very rapidly alternate between the notes indicated by continuously hammering on and pulling off.

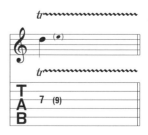

TAPPING: Hammer ("tap") the fret indicated with the pick-hand index or middle finger and pull off to the note fretted by the fret hand.

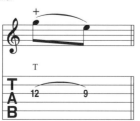

NATURAL HARMONIC: Strike the note while the fret-hand lightly touches the string directly over the fret indicated.

PINCH HARMONIC: The note is fretted normally and a harmonic is produced by adding the edge of the thumb or the tip of the index finger of the pick hand to the normal pick attack.

HARP HARMONIC: The note is fretted normally and a harmonic is produced by gently resting the pick hand's index finger directly above the indicated fret (in parentheses) while the pick hand's thumb or pick assists by plucking the appropriate string.

PICK SCRAPE: The edge of the pick is rubbed down (or up) the string, producing a scratchy sound.

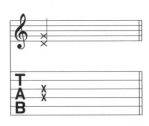

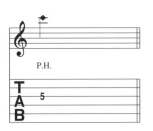

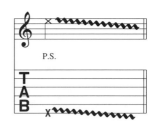

MUFFLED STRINGS: A percussive sound is produced by laying the fret hand across the string(s) without depressing, and striking them with the pick hand.

PALM MUTING: The note is partially muted by the pick hand lightly touching the string(s) just before the bridge.

RAKE: Drag the pick across the strings indicated with a single motion.

TREMOLO PICKING: The note is picked as rapidly and continuously as possible.

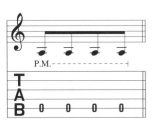

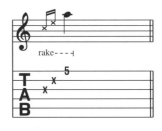

ARPEGGIATE: Play the notes of the chord indicated by quickly rolling them from bottom to top.

VIBRATO BAR DIVE AND RETURN: The pitch of the note or chord is dropped a specified number of steps (in rhythm) then returned to the original pitch.

VIBRATO BAR SCOOP: Depress the bar just before striking the note, then quickly release the bar.

VIBRATO BAR DIP: Strike the note and then immediately drop a specified number of steps, then release back to the original pitch.

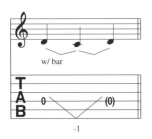

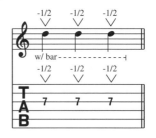

Additional Musical Definitions

(accent)	• Accentuate note (play it louder)	
(accent)	• Accentuate note with great intensity	
(staccato)	• Play the note short	
	• Downstroke	
∨	• Upstroke	

Rhy. Fig. • Label used to recall a recurring accompaniment pattern (usually chordal).

Riff • Label used to recall composed, melodic lines (usually single notes) which recur.

Fill • Label used to identify a brief melodic figure which is to be inserted into the arrangement.

Rhy. Fill • A chordal version of a Fill.

tacet • Instrument is silent (drops out).

D.S. al Coda • Go back to the sign (𝄋), then play until the measure marked "**To Coda**," then skip to the section labelled "**Coda**."

D.C. al Fine • Go back to the beginning of the song and play until the measure marked "**Fine**" (end).

• Repeat measures between signs.

• When a repeated section has different endings, play the first ending only the first time and the second ending only the second time.

NOTE: Tablature numbers in parentheses mean:
1. The note is being sustained over a system (note in standard notation is tied), or
2. The note is sustained, but a new articulation (such as a hammer-on, pull-off, slide or vibrato begins), or
3. The note is a barely audible "ghost" note (note in standard notation is also in parentheses).

THE DECADE SERIES

These collections, especially for guitarists, feature the top tunes that shaped a decade, transcribed note-for-note.

The 1950s

35 pivotal songs from the early rock years: All Shook Up • Be-Bop-a-Lula • Bo Diddley • Boppin' the Blues • Cannonball • Donna • Foggy Mountain Breakdown • Get Rhythm • Guitar Boogie Shuffle • Heartbreak Hotel • Hound Dog • I'm Lookin' for Someone to Love • I'm Movin' On • I'm Your Hoochie Coochie Man • Lonesome Town • Matchbox • Moonlight in Vermont • My Babe • Poor Little Fool • Put Your Cat Clothes On • Race With the Devil • Rebel 'Rouser • Reconsider Baby • Rock Around the Clock • Rocket '88 • Rockin' Robin • Sleepwalk • Slippin' and Slidin' • Susie-Q • Sweet Little Angel • Tequila • (They Call It) Stormy Monday (Stormy Monday Blues) • Wake Up Little Susie • The World Is Waiting for the Sunrise • Yankee Doodle Dixie

_____00690543 Guitar Recorded Versions $14.95

The 1960s

30 songs that defined the '60s: Badge • Blackbird • Fun, Fun, Fun • Gloria • Good Lovin' • Green Onions • Happy Together • Hello Mary Lou • Hey Joe • Hush • I Can See for Miles • I Feel Fine • I Get Around • In the Midnight Hour • Jingo (Jin-Go-Lo-Ba) • Let's Live for Today • Louie, Louie • My Girl • Oh, Pretty Woman • On the Road Again • The Promised Land • Somebody to Love • Soul Man • Suite: Judy Blue Eyes • Susie-Q • Time Is on My Side • (So) Tired of Waiting for You • Train Kept A-Rollin' • Walk Don't Run • Wild Thing

_____00690542 Guitar Recorded Versions $14.95

The 1970s

30 top songs from the '70s: Barracuda • Best of My Love • Blue Collar Man (Long Nights) • Breakdown • Burning Love • Dust in the Wind • Evil Woman • Freeway Jam • Godzilla • Happy • Landslide • Lay Down Sally • Let It Be • Maggie May • No Woman No Cry • Oye Como Va • Paranoid • Rock and Roll Hoochie Koo • Show Me the Way • Smoke on the Water • So Into You • Space Oddity • Stayin' Alive • Teach Your Children • Time in a Bottle • Walk This Way • Wheel in the Sky • You Ain't Seen Nothin' Yet • You Really Got Me • You've Got a Friend

_____00690541 Guitar Recorded Versions $15.95

The 1980s

30 songs that best represent the decade: Caught Up in You • Down Boys • 867-5309/Jenny • Every Breath You Take • Eye of the Tiger • Fight for Your Right (To Party) • Heart and Soul • Hit Me With Your Best Shot • I Love Rock 'N Roll • In and Out of Love • La Bamba • Land of Confusion • Love Struck Baby • (Bang Your Head) Metal Health • Money for Nothing • Mony, Mony • Rag Doll • Refugee • R.O.C.K. in the U.S.A. (A Salute to '60s Rock) • Rock Me • Rock You Like a Hurricane • Running on Faith • Seventeen • Start Me Up • Summer of '69 • Sweet Child O' Mine • Wait • What I Like About You • Working for the Weekend • You May Be Right

_____00690540 Guitar Recorded Versions $15.95

The 1990s

30 essential '90s classics: All I Wanna Do • Are You Gonna Go My Way • Barely Breathing • Blue on Black • Boot Scootin' Boogie • Building a Mystery • Bulls on Parade • Come Out and Play • Cryin' • (Everything I Do) I Do It for You • Fields of Gold • Free As a Bird • Friends in Low Places • Give Me One Reason • Hold My Hand • I Can't Dance • I'm the Only One • The Impression That I Get • Iris • Jump, Jive an' Wail • More Than Words • Santa Monica • Semi-Charmed Life • Silent Lucidity • Smells Like Teen Spirit • Smooth • Tears in Heaven • Two Princes • Under the Bridge • Wonderwall

_____00690539 Guitar Recorded Versions $15.95

FOR MORE INFORMATION, SEE YOUR LOCAL MUSIC DEALER,
OR WRITE TO:

7777 W. BLUEMOUND RD. P.O. BOX 13819 MILWAUKEE, WI 53213

Prices, contents and availability subject to change without notice.

www.halleonard.com

RECORDED VERSIONS
The Best Note-For-Note Transcriptions Available

RECORDED VERSIONS GUITAR

ALL BOOKS INCLUDE TABLATURE

00690016 Will Ackerman Collection $19.95	00690127 Goo Goo Dolls – A Boy Named Goo $19.95	00690395 Rage Against The Machine –
00690146 Aerosmith – Toys in the Attic $19.95	00690338 Goo Goo Dolls – Dizzy Up the Girl $19.95	The Battle of Los Angeles ....$
00694865 Alice In Chains – Dirt $19.95	00690117 John Gorka Collection $19.95	00690145 Rage Against The Machine – Evil Empire ..$
00694932 Allman Brothers Band – Volume 1 ....$24.95	00690114 Buddy Guy Collection Vol. A-J $22.95	00690179 Rancid – And Out Come the Wolves .....$
00694933 Allman Brothers Band – Volume 2 .....$24.95	00690193 Buddy Guy Collection Vol. L-Y $22.95	00690055 Red Hot Chili Peppers –
00694934 Allman Brothers Band – Volume 3 .....$24.95	00694798 George Harrison Anthology $19.95	Bloodsugarsexmagik ....$
00694877 Chet Atkins – Guitars For All Seasons $19.95	00690068 Return Of The Hellecasters $19.95	00690379 Red Hot Chili Peppers – Californication ..$
00690418 Best of Audio Adrenaline $17.95	00692930 Jimi Hendrix – Are You Experienced? ...$24.95	00690090 Red Hot Chili Peppers – One Hot Minute ..$
00694918 Randy Bachman Collection $22.95	00692931 Jimi Hendrix – Axis: Bold As Love $22.95	00694937 Jimmy Reed – Master Bluesman ....$
00690366 Bad Company Original Anthology - Bk 1 ..$19.95	00692932 Jimi Hendrix – Electric Ladyland $24.95	00694899 R.E.M. – Automatic For The People ....$
00690367 Bad Company Original Anthology - Bk 2 ..$19.95	00692218 Jimi Hendrix – First Rays of the New Rising Sun $27.95	00690260 Jimmie Rodgers Guitar Collection .....$
00694880 Beatles – Abbey Road $19.95	00690038 Gary Hoey – Best Of $19.95	00690014 Rolling Stones – Exile On Main Street ...$
00694863 Beatles –	00660029 Buddy Holly $19.95	00690186 Rolling Stones – Rock & Roll Circus .....$
Sgt. Pepper's Lonely Hearts Club Band ..$19.95	00660169 John Lee Hooker – A Blues Legend $19.95	00690135 Otis Rush Collection ....$
00690383 Beatles – Yellow Submarine $19.95	00690054 Hootie & The Blowfish –	00690031 Santana's Greatest Hits ....$
00690174 Beck – Mellow Gold $17.95	Cracked Rear View $19.95	00690150 Son Seals – Bad Axe Blues ....$
00690346 Beck – Mutations $19.95	00694905 Howlin' Wolf $19.95	00690128 Seven Mary Three – American Standards ..$
00690175 Beck – Odelay $17.95	00690136 Indigo Girls – 1200 Curfews $22.95	00120105 Kenny Wayne Shepherd – Ledbetter Heights $
00694884 The Best of George Benson $19.95	00694938 Elmore James –	00120123 Kenny Wayne Shepherd – Trouble Is ...$
00692385 Chuck Berry $19.95	Master Electric Slide Guitar $19.95	00690196 Silverchair – Freak Show ....$
00692200 Black Sabbath –	00690167 Skip James Blues Guitar Collection $16.95	00690130 Silverchair – Frogstomp ....$
We Sold Our Soul For Rock 'N' Roll ..$19.95	00694833 Billy Joel For Guitar $19.95	00690041 Smithereens – Best Of ....$
00690115 Blind Melon – Soup $19.95	00694912 Eric Johnson – Ah Via Musicom $19.95	00690385 Sonicflood ....$
00690305 Blink 182 – Dude Ranch $19.95	00690169 Eric Johnson – Venus Isle $22.95	00694885 Spin Doctors – Pocket Full Of Kryptonite ..$
00690028 Blue Oyster Cult – Cult Classics $19.95	00694799 Robert Johnson – At The Crossroads $19.95	00694921 Steppenwolf, The Best Of ....$
00690219 Blur $19.95	00693185 Judas Priest – Vintage Hits $19.95	00694957 Rod Stewart – Acoustic Live ....$
00690168 Roy Buchanon Collection $19.95	00690277 Best of Kansas $19.95	00690021 Sting – Fields Of Gold ....$
00690364 Cake – Songbook $19.95	00690073 B. B. King – 1950-1957 ....$24.95	00690242 Suede – Coming Up ....$
00690337 Jerry Cantrell – Boggy Depot $19.95	00690098 B. B. King – 1958-1967 ....$24.95	00694824 Best Of James Taylor ....$
00690293 Best of Steven Curtis Chapman $19.95	00690444 B.B. King and Eric Clapton –	00690238 Third Eye Blind ....$
00690043 Cheap Trick – Best Of $19.95	Riding with the King $19.95	00690403 Third Eye Blind – Blue ....$
00690171 Chicago – Definitive Guitar Collection ..$22.95	00690134 Freddie King Collection $17.95	00690267 311 ....$
00690415 Clapton Chronicles – Best of Eric Clapton ..$17.95	00690157 Kiss – Alive $19.95	00690030 Toad The Wet Sprocket ....$
00690393 Eric Clapton – Selections from Blues ...$19.95	00690163 Mark Knopfler/Chet Atkins – Neck and Neck $19.95	00690228 Tonic – Lemon Parade ....$
00660139 Eric Clapton – Journeyman $19.95	00690296 Patty Larkin Songbook $17.95	00690295 Tool – Aenima ....$
00694869 Eric Clapton – Live Acoustic $19.95	00690018 Living Colour – Best Of $19.95	00690039 Steve Vai – Alien Love Secrets ....$
00694896 John Mayall/Eric Clapton – Bluesbreakers $19.95	00694845 Yngwie Malmsteen – Fire And Ice $19.95	00690172 Steve Vai – Fire Garden ....$
00690162 Best of the Clash $19.95	00694956 Bob Marley – Legend $19.95	00690023 Jimmie Vaughan – Strange Pleasures ..$
00690166 Albert Collins – The Alligator Years $16.95	00690283 Best of Sarah McLachlan $19.95	00690370 Stevie Ray Vaughan and Double Trouble –
00694940 Counting Crows – August & Everything After $19.95	00690382 Sarah McLachlan – Mirrorball $19.95	The Real Deal: Greatest Hits Volume 2 ....$
00690197 Counting Crows – Recovering the Satellites ..$19.95	00690354 Sarah McLachlan – Surfacing $19.95	00690455 Stevie Ray Vaughan – Blues at Sunrise ..$
00694840 Cream – Disraeli Gears $19.95	00690442 Matchbox 20 – Mad Season $19.95	00660136 Stevie Ray Vaughan – In Step ....$
00690401 Creed – Human Clay $19.95	00690239 Matchbox 20 – Yourself or Someone Like You ..$19.95	00690417 Stevie Ray Vaughan – Live at Carnegie Hall $
00690352 Creed – My Own Prison $19.95	00690244 Megadeath – Cryptic Writings $19.95	00694835 Stevie Ray Vaughan – The Sky Is Crying ..$
00690184 dc Talk – Jesus Freak $19.95	00690236 Mighty Mighty Bosstones – Let's Face It ..$19.95	00694776 Vaughan Brothers – Family Style .....$
00690333 dc Talk – Supernatural $19.95	00690040 Steve Miller Band Greatest Hits $19.95	00120026 Joe Walsh – Look What I Did... ......$
00660186 Alex De Grassi Guitar Collection $19.95	00694802 Gary Moore – Still Got The Blues $19.95	00694789 Muddy Waters – Deep Blues ....$
00690289 Best of Deep Purple $17.95	00694958 Mountain, Best Of $19.95	00690071 Weezer ....$
00694831 Derek And The Dominos –	00690448 MxPx – The Ever Passing Moment $19.95	00690286 Weezer – Pinkerton ....$
Layla & Other Assorted Love Songs $19.95	00694913 Nirvana – In Utero $19.95	00690447 Who, The – Best of ....$
00690322 Ani Di Franco – Little Plastic Castle $19.95	00694883 Nirvana – Nevermind $19.95	00694970 Who, The – Definitive Collection A-E ...$
00690187 Dire Straits – Brothers In Arms $19.95	00690026 Nirvana – Acoustic In New York $19.95	00694971 Who, The – Definitive Collection F-Li ...$
00690191 Dire Straits – Money For Nothing $24.95	00690121 Oasis – (What's The Story) Morning Glory $19.95	00694972 Who, The – Definitive Collection Lo-R ...$
00695382 The Very Best of Dire Straits –	00690204 Offspring, The – Ixnay on the Hombre ..$17.95	00694973 Who, The – Definitive Collection S-Y ...$
Sultans of Swing $19.95	00690203 Offspring, The – Smash $17.95	00690319 Stevie Wonder Hits ....$
00660178 Willie Dixon – Master Blues Composer ..$24.95	00694830 Ozzy Osbourne – No More Tears $19.95	
00690250 Best of Duane Eddy $16.95	00694855 Pearl Jam – Ten $19.95	
00690349 Eve 6 ....$19.95	00690053 Liz Phair – Whip Smart $19.95	
00313164 Eve 6 – Horrorscope $19.95	00690176 Phish – Billy Breathes $22.95	
00690323 Fastball – All the Pain Money Can Buy ..$19.95	00690424 Phish – Farmhouse $19.95	
00690089 Foo Fighters $19.95	00690331 Phish – The Story of Ghost $19.95	
00690235 Foo Fighters – The Colour and the Shape ..$19.95	00690428 Pink Floyd – Dark Side of the Moon ...$19.95	
00690394 Foo Fighters –	00693800 Pink Floyd – Early Classics $19.95	
There Is Nothing Left to Lose $19.95	00690456 P.O.D. – The Fundamental	
00690222 G3 Live – Satriani, Vai, Johnson $22.95	Elements of Southtown $19.95	
00694807 Danny Gatton – 88 Elmira St $19.95	00694967 Police – Message In A Box Boxed Set ...$70.00	
00690438 Genesis Guitar Anthology $19.95	00694974 Queen – A Night At The Opera $19.95	

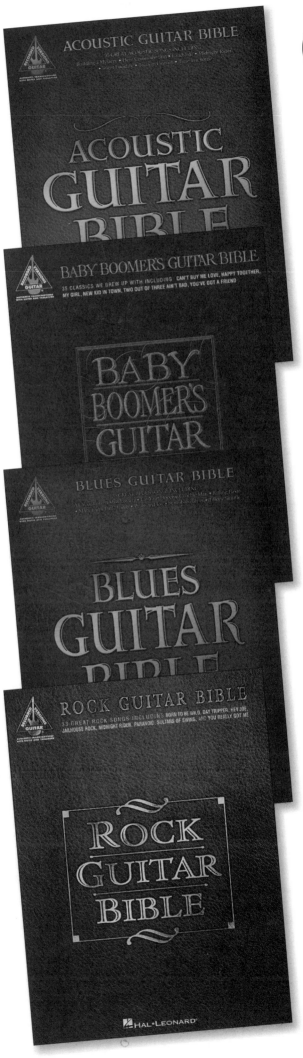

GUITAR BIBLES

from

HAL•LEONARD®

*Hal Leonard proudly presents the Guitar Bible series.
Each volume contains best-selling songs in authentic,
note-for-note transcriptions with notes and tablature. $19.95 each*

ACOUSTIC GUITAR BIBLE

35 essential classics for those who prefer acoustic guitar. Songs include: Angie • Building a Mystery • Change the World • Dust in the Wind • Here Comes the Sun • Hold My Hand • Iris • Leaving on a Jet Plane • Maggie May • The Man Who Sold the World • Southern Cross • Tears in Heaven • Wild World • You Were Meant for Me • and more.
_____00690432

BABY BOOMER'S GUITAR BIBLE

Note-for-note transcriptions for 35 crown-jewel classics from rock 'n' roll's greatest era. Includes: Angie • Can't Buy Me Love • Happy Together • Hey Jude • I Heard It Through the Grapevine • Imagine • It's Still Rock and Roll to Me • Laughing • Longer • My Girl • New Kid in Town • Rebel, Rebel • Two Out of Three Ain't Bad • Wild Thing • Wonderful Tonight • and more.
_____00690412

BLUES GUITAR BIBLE

The only book of the blues you need. 35 exact transcriptions of such classics as: All Your Love (I Miss Loving) • Boom Boom • Everyday (I Have the Blues) • Hide Away • I Can't Quit You Baby • I'm Your Hoochie Coochie Man • Killing Floor • Kind Hearted Woman Blues • Mary Had a Little Lamb • Pride and Joy • Sweet Little Angel • The Things That I Used to Do • The Thrill Is Gone • and more.
_____00690437

BLUES-ROCK GUITAR BIBLE

The definitive collection of 35 note-for-note guitar transcriptions, including: Bad Love • Black Hearted Woman • Blue on Black • Boom Boom (Out Go the Lights) • Couldn't Stand the Weather • Cross Road Blues (Crossroads) • Hide Away • The House Is Rockin' • Killing Floor • Love Struck Baby • Move It on Over • Piece of My Heart • Statesboro Blues • Still Got the Blues • Train Kept a Rollin' • You Shook Me • and more.
_____00690450

COUNTRY GUITAR BIBLE

35 revered country classics in one hefty collection, including: Ain't Goin' Down ('Til the Sun Comes Up) • Blue Eyes Crying in the Rain • Boot Scootin' Boogie • Friends in Low Places • I'm So Lonesome I Could Cry • My Baby Thinks He's a Train • T-R-O-U-B-L-E • and more.
_____00690465

FOLK-ROCK GUITAR BIBLE

35 essential folk-rock guitar favorites, including: At Seventeen • Blackbird • Do You Believe in Magic • Fire and Rain • Happy Together • Here Comes the Sun • Leaving on a Jet Plane • Me and Bobby McGee • Our House • Time in a Bottle • Turn! Turn! Turn! (To Everything There Is a Season) • You've Got a Friend • and more.
_____00690464

HARD ROCK GUITAR BIBLE

The essential collection of 35 hard rock classics, including: Back in the Saddle • Ballroom Blitz • Bang a Gong (Get It On) • Barracuda • Fight the Good Fight • Hair of the Dog • Living After Midnight • Rock You like a Hurricane • School's Out • Stone Cold Crazy • War Pigs • Welcome to the Jungle • You Give Love a Bad Name • and more.
_____00690453

JAZZ GUITAR BIBLE

The one book that has all of the jazz guitar classics transcribed note-for-note, with standard notation and tablature. Includes over 30 songs: Body and Soul • Girl Talk • I'll Remember April • In a Sentimental Mood • My Funny Valentine • Nuages • Satin Doll • So What • Star Dust • Take Five • Tangerine • Yardbird Suite • and more.
_____00690466

R&B GUITAR BIBLE

A divine collection of 35 R&B classics, including: Brick House • Dancing in the Street • Fire • I Can't Help Myself (Sugar Pie, Honey Bunch) • I Got You (I Feel Good) • I Heard It Through the Grapevine • Love Rollercoaster • My Girl • Papa's Got a Brand New Bag • Shining Star • Sir Duke • Super Freak • (Your Love Keeps Lifting Me) Higher and Higher • and more.
_____00690452

ROCK GUITAR BIBLE

Exact transcriptions in notes and tab of 33 essential rock songs: All Day and All of the Night • Born to Be Wild • Day Tripper • Gloria • Hey Joe • Jailhouse Rock • Midnight Rider • Money • Paranoid • Sultans of Swing • Walk This Way • You Really Got Me • more!
_____00690313

Prices, contents, and availability subject to change without notice.

www.halleonard.com

0101

GET BETTER AT GUITAR

...with These Great Guitar Instruction Books from Hal Leonard!

DON'T FRET NOTE MAP

REVOLUTIONARY GUITAR FINGER POSITIONING GUIDE
• created by Nicholas Ravagni

It's never been easier to learn to play guitar! For beginners just starting out or experienced guitarists who want to learn to read music, the *Don't Fret Note Map*™ will give players the tools they need to locate notes on the guitar. This revolutionary finger positioning guide fits all electric and acoustic guitars with no adhesive or fasteners, shows the note names and locations all over the fretboard and uses a unique color-coded method to make note-reading easy. The accompanying booklet includes full instructions and four easy songs to let players practice their new-found skills!

_____00695587 ....$9.95

Also available:
DON'T FRET CHORD MAP™

REVOLUTIONARY GUITAR FINGER POSITIONING GUIDE
• created by Nicholas Ravagni

_____00695670 ....$9.95

GUITAR DIAL 9-1-1

50 WAYS TO IMPROVE YOUR PLAYING ... NOW!! • *by Ken Parille*

Need to breathe new life into your guitar playing? This book is your admission into the Guitar ER! You'll learn to: expand your harmonic vocabulary; improvise with chromatic notes; create rhythmic diversity; improve your agility through helpful drills; supply soulful fills; create melodic lines through chord changes; and much more! The accompanying CD includes 99 demonstration tracks.

_____00695405 Book/CD Pack.............................$16.95

GUITAR TECHNIQUES • *by Michael Mueller*

Guitar Techniques is a terrific reference and teaching companion, as it clearly defines and demonstrates how to properly execute cool moves ranging from bending, vibrato and legato to tapping, whammy bar and playing with your teeth! The CD contains 92 demonstration tracks in country, rock, pop and jazz styles. Essential techniques covered include: Fretting • Strumming • Trills • Picking • Vibrato • Tapping • Bends • Harmonics • Muting • Slides • and more.

_____00695562 Book/CD Pack.............................$14.95

THE GUITARIST'S SURVIVAL KIT

EVERYTHING YOU NEED TO KNOW TO BE A WORKING MUSICIAN
• *by Dale Turner*

From repertoire to accompaniment patterns to licks, this book is fully stocked to give you the confidence knowing you can "get by" and survive, regardless of the situation. The book covers: songs and set lists; gear; rhythm riffs in styles from blues to funk to rock to metal; lead licks in blues, country, jazz & rock styles; transposition and more. The CD features 99 demonstration tracks, and the book includes standard notation and tab.

_____00695380 Book/CD Pack.............................$14.95

LEFT-HANDED GUITAR

THE COMPLETE METHOD • *by Troy Stetina*

Attention all Southpaws: it's time to turn your playing around! We're proud to announce that our groundbreaking guitar method solely devoted to lefties is now available with a CD! Complete with photos, diagrams and grids designed especially for the left-handed player, this book/CD pack teaches fundamentals such as: chords, scales, riffs, strumming; rock, blues, fingerpicking and other styles; tuning and theory; reading standard notation and tablature; and much more!

_____00695630 Book/CD Pack...................................$14.95
_____00695247 Book Only $9.95

PICTURE CHORD ENCYCLOPEDIA

PHOTOS & DIAGRAMS FOR 2,600 GUITAR CHORDS!

The most comprehensive guitar chord resource ever! Beginning with helpful notes on how to use the book, how to choose the best voicings and how to construct chords, this extensive, 272-page source for all playing styles and levels features five easy-to-play voicings of 44 chord qualities for each of the twelve musical keys – 2,640 chords in all! For each, there is a clearly illustrated chord frame, as well as *an actual photo* of the chord being played! Includes info on basic fingering principles, open chords and barre chords, partial chords and broken-set forms, and more. Great for all guitarists!

_____00695224 ....$19.95

SCALE CHORD RELATIONSHIPS

A GUIDE TO KNOWING WHAT NOTES TO PLAY – AND WHY!
• *by Michael Mueller & Jeff Schroedl*

Scale Chord Relationships teaches players how to determine which scales to play with which chords, so guitarists will never have to fear chord changes again! This book/CD pack explains how to: recognize keys; analyze chord progressions; use the modes; play over nondiatonic harmony; use harmonic and melodic minor scales; use symmetrical scales such as chromatic, whole-tone and diminished scales; incorporate exotic scales such as Hungarian major and Gypsy minor; and much more!

_____00695563 Book/CD Pack...................................$14.95

FOR MORE INFORMATION, SEE YOUR LOCAL MUSIC DEALER, OR WRITE TO:

HAL•LEONARD® CORPORATION

7777 W. BLUEMOUND RD. P.O. BOX 13819 MILWAUKEE, WI 53213

Visit Hal Leonard Online at
www.halleonard.com

PRICES, CONTENTS AND AVAILABILITY SUBJECT TO CHANGE WITHOUT NOTICE.

7-STRING GUITAR

AN ALL-PURPOSE REFERENCE FOR NAVIGATING YOUR FRETBOARD
• *by Andy Martin*

Introducing *7-String Guitar*, the first-ever method book written especially for seven-stringed instruments. It teaches chords, scales and arpeggios, all as they are adapted for the 7-string guitar. It features helpful fingerboard charts, and riffs & licks in standard notation and tablature to help players expand their sonic range in any style of music. It also includes an introduction by and biography of the author, tips on how to approach the book, a guitar notation legend, and much more!

_____00695508 ....$12.95

TOTAL ROCK GUITAR

A COMPLETE GUIDE TO LEARNING ROCK GUITAR • *by Troy Stetina*

Total Rock Guitar is a unique and comprehensive source for learning rock guitar, designed to develop both lead and rhythm playing. This book/CD pack covers: getting a tone that rocks; open chords, power chords and barre chords; riffs, scales and licks; string bending, strumming, palm muting, harmonics and alternate picking; all rock styles; and much more. The examples in the book are in standard notation with chord grids and tablature, and the CD includes full-band backing for all 22 songs.

_____00695246 Book/CD Pack...................................$17.95

THE GUITAR F/X COOKBOOK

• *by Chris Amelar*

The ultimate source for guitar tricks, effects, and other unorthodox techniques. This book demonstrates and explains 45 incredible guitar sounds using common stomp boxes and a few unique techniques, including: pick scraping, police siren, ghost slide, church bell, jaw harp, delay swells, looping, monkey's scream, cat's meow, race car, pickup tapping, and much more.

_____00695080 Book/CD Pack...................................$14.95

BLUES YOU CAN USE

• *by John Ganapes*

A comprehensive source designed to help guitarists develop both lead and rhythm playing. Covers: Texas, Delta, R&B, early rock and roll, gospel, blues/rock and more. Includes 21 complete solos; chord progressions and riffs; turnarounds; moveable scales and more. CD features leads and full band backing.

_____00695007 Book/CD Pack...................................$19.95

JAZZ RHYTHM GUITAR

THE COMPLETE GUIDE • *by Jack Grassel*

This book/CD pack by award-winning guitarist and distinguished teacher Jack Grassel will help rhythm guitarists better understand: chord symbols and voicings; comping styles and patterns; equipment, accessories and set-up; the fingerboard; chord theory; and much more. The accompanying CD includes 74 full-band tracks.

_____00695654 Book/CD Pack...................................$19.95